NAVIGATING THE DARKNESS

NAVIGATING THE DARKNESS

EMERGING AS LIGHT

V. Marie

APRIL 14, 2017

ISBN: 1545389527
ISBN 13: 9781545389522

CONTENTS

ACKNOWLEDGMENTS

I WANT TO dedicate this book to my parents first and foremost.

- To my mother, Melody who earned every gray hair she has from me, I am sure. You taught me how to love when others did not love me, to have compassion for those who showed none for others, acceptance when I felt rejected, mercy for those who starved for it and grace for others in the amount in which I wanted to receive it for myself. You emulated Jesus in every way. You loved me when I was hard to love. I admire and respect the years of arduous work and struggles you had as a single parent raising five kids. I love you very much. You believed in me when I did not believe in myself. My biggest fan and encourager. You were and are the best mom ever!
- To my dad Leslie II, though you are deceased from this life, you were a strong encourager of me writing this book. We had tough times as a father and daughter, until later years. I finally realized that you were the one that taught me to stand up for what I believed in. For so long I thought that you argued with me because you thought I was always wrong. It was not until months before your death that you explained that you chose the opposing side to every conversation to teach me to debate my beliefs passionately. It has served me well through the years and it has helped me

to stand up for my Lord Jesus Christ when I may have been fearful to do so otherwise. I love and miss you terribly and am so thankful that you chose me!

- To my husband Michael, thank you for your encouragement and the words we jokingly said nearly every day for three years, "write the book". The words were seeds planted and I love and appreciate you. Together we will answer His call.
- To my sons, Duley and Dalton who are the apples of my eye. Thank you both for your steadfast love and loyalty. My heart swells with humility and pride for the Godly men you have grown up to be. We have been through some tough years together, but love and family prevailed. Lessons were learned along the way and we are all three better for it. I am thankful for my stepdaughter Kenzi, a sweet joy in my life. And to the wonderful half-siblings of my sons who all share the same father, Hope and Dylan, we were all connected by a common denominator. I love you both. We all grew from the same story. I was proud to be your step mother for a time and a step grandmother to your children. Love to my daughters-in-law Rachel and Brianna.
- To my grandchildren who have given me purpose in my older years and fulfilled my desire for a huge family. Kameron, Kaylee, Kade, Reid, Zachary, Brayden, Astrid (deceased), Kaelynn, Quintynn, Brooklyn, Remy, Raegan, Leila, Duley Jr., Owen, Dylan, Lyla, Easton, Reese, Syanna, Lanedyn and baby Averi, I love you all. To God I am thankful for every one of you. My prayer is that as individuals that you will each heed the call of God and fulfill His will in your lives. My hope is that every one of you will accept Jesus as your Savior and that you will love Him more today than you did yesterday and spread that love with everyone you meet.

- To my biological father John, who I recently (two years ago) found for the first time. Though up to this point we still have not met, you have been faithful to call me and we have caught up on 50 plus years we never had. You came into my life in a strategically, God initiated way, at a time when my dad had died and I was not coping well. You helped me through the grief by being a father figure to me when I needed my dad so badly. I honor and respect you for the man you have become and for being in my life now.
- To Teresa Gorman my pastor's wife who for a full year would pray for me and would tell me to "pick it up" which meant, take on the task of writing the book. These words "Pick it up" came from a visiting youth pastor who called me out with a word of knowledge. Pastor T., thank you for hearing a voice from God and sharing it with me. Teresa also edited my book for which I am grateful! Thank you for the many hours you spent doing this.
- To my siblings who have collectively all shared a deep abiding love for one another. It was that very love that kept us all a float and helped us survive the hard times in life. We learned we were stronger when we merged forces together to help one another. Leslie III, Ruth, Gail, David, Wendy and Robert, and my step siblings, Tonya, Michael and Kelly, I love you all very much! I am thankful you are my siblings. To the siblings, I have yet to meet and hope someday to be so fortunate, John, Jason and Adam I look forward to growing in relationship with you.
- Thanks to Dave Waggoner for the challenging work and effort doing the graphic design for the book cover. Much love to you!

- To the LIFE SKILLS GANG: Lindsay, Ruth, Les, Mary, Rebecca, Suzanne, Michele, Holly, Tim, Dave, LaShelle, Greta, Jerry, Carolyn, The Crossroads Church, Pastor Ron Bowell whom I love and respect, and so many others too numerous to name that came in and out through the years of our teaching the Life Skills Program by helping to facilitate classes. I could have never lived the dream or taught so many people had I not had you there to help facilitate or in other positions as needed. God will credit your account in heaven, I am sure. Pastor Jeff Piepho, your help in making us get the message to the teenagers via electronics with your dramatic, dynamic personality helped to touch so many lives! **Lindsay**, you were my right arm. Some special thanks for all you did for me and so many others. Thank you one and all!
- Thank you to my Lord God who has never given up on me and has been patient beyond reason. I love you. My prayer is that you will use this work of love to guide others into your Kingdom and that all the Glory be yours today and every day. Amen.

FOREWORD

NAVIGATING THE DARKNESS

We live in perilous times. For years, many people have struggled with depression, sadness, feeling out of control of their lives with a sense of hopelessness and despair. However, it appears current days are far worse than I have ever seen in my lifetime. With the way, the world is evolving into utter chaos, hate and instability, it leaves our futures hanging in a balance of which we cannot determine the outcome. Fear becomes a primary emotion that many share.

When our lives appear to be held in the hands of others and control of the freedoms we have been accustomed to are threatened, it can leave us with feelings of high anxiety and for some people, feelings of hopelessness and helplessness. We do not know what to do. We wonder if there is anything that we can do or if there is anything that can be done. Without position, power or money it appears there is nothing that one person can do to make a difference in all this mess. The Bible says that hope deferred makes the heart sick, but it also says that if we place our hope in the Lord we no longer need to fear the unknown for it is in God's hands and He knows the future. We need to learn to trust Him.

Paralyzed by our individual fears of the unknown future that we may face, many people sit and simply wait to see what may happen, others scream out with rage, anger and violence, while yet others retreat quietly laying everything in the hands of the Lord and simply pray. More people now than ever before have had an increase in depression, addictions and mental illness due to the overwhelming issues that they are faced with every day in these uncertain times. Their minds are full of questions, doubts, out of control emotions such as worry, anxiety and the primary one, fear. Numerous situations in their lives that they struggle with leaves them feeling without the possibility of resolve or hope for a future. My desire is that I can prove that there is hope for you and for me.

When I first started working on the inpatient psychiatric unit in the late 1980's on a 15-bed facility it was rare to be full. The average patient care load for a nurse then was 4 to 6 patients and many times a nurse would be called off for low census due to lack of patients to care for. Now, in 2017 the 19-bed inpatient unit is full, with a waiting list. The hospital scrambles to increase the size of the unit to accommodate the ever-increasing need. Overtime is the norm for most nurses. There are not enough nurses to take care of the need we are facing in this nation between mental illness and drug addiction. Much of which is directly related to the inability to cope with life in general. Depression, anxiety and drugs circle one another repeatedly. We must stop this cycle together.

For years, I have been teaching psycho-educational classes on relationships and life skills application to help others to overcome some of these very issues I speak of here. I began a quest to teach because I care about people and I struggled with these same issues. To find healing for my past hurts, I took classes to face the root cause of my pain so that I could change the course of direction for my future. This is very scary to do. Self-reflection and evaluation is hard to face. It is even more difficult to change what you have discovered about yourself. It means accepting responsibility for your part in the situation. It means stopping the blame shifting of all your problems onto other people, things and illnesses. It means self-accountability to change what we can in our lives. We must accept some responsibility for our wellness. Excuses must go out the window. No more excuses!

When I found some of the foundational answers that I needed to make changes in my life, it gave me a platform from which to grow and pivot. I did not have all the answers that I thought that I needed, so I pressed onward and continued my daily search. I still search for answers even today, because I will never have all the answers. I still have struggles. I will never be a perfect person in this world. I sometimes regress and I fall. I just get back up and try again. I have found that I do not have to look as far and as wide as I once did for answers so desperately, because the Lord rescued me. He gave me His Word in book form to function as my search engine. It is called the Holy Bible. Without it I am lost.

Before God stepped into my life I had studied and tarried in various directions looking for answers. At times, I became confused and felt that my life would never be on track. I was wrong of course. I just needed to stay focused on the goal and have the tenacity to not give up. Lacking some of the character traits that I needed to achieve my goals slowed me down many times. It was in those times of what I call the desert, that I grew the most and matured the character traits that I needed to move to the next level or stage in my life. At this current stage in my life, I am a firm believer that every bump in the road we experience is in preparation for the next bump we are about to experience. It is a test. Without the last bump, we cannot effectively have victory of the next bump because we will lack the knowledge and tools to cope and succeed.

I had the Lord in most of my life in many ways. My immaturity in my relationship with Him did not allow me to recognize His presence at times or to afford me the answers I was seeking. It was not until my relationship with Him began to grow that I truly started learning. I needed to mature first, to recognize where I was in life and in my relationship with Christ. In fact, I needed to learn who I was in Christ. I had to be real with myself. I had to be honest if I ever wanted to grow and mature in my emotional development and spiritual maturity. They go hand in hand.

What are the desert times you might ask? It is a replicated time of the Israelites journey in the wilderness. When the Israelites were freed from bondage in Egypt they were to follow Moses to the Promised Land. But though they had been freed physically from bondage they were not mentally freed from their bondage. They lacked the faith in God's ability to take them all the way to the Promise Land that God had given them. This caused them to self-sabotage which prevented them from entering the Promised Land, sooner than they did.

Because of their own self destructive choices and lack of faith, they wandered in the desert for forty years and many died there never receiving what God wanted so badly to give them! They did not receive, not because God didn't want them to have it. On the contrary, they did not receive because they would not be obedient to God's instruction. They did not trust God. They lacked faith. They would not listen to their leader Moses whom God had provided for them. They would not give up their past. They would not accept the gift from the Lord and follow the path to receive it. Ultimately, they were not faithful to the love of the Lord and their relationship and could not receive the love He was raining upon them. How many times have we done this in our own lives? Too many times, I must admit for myself. I have sabotaged more good things in my life than I care to count. Many times, I did not feel that I deserved it or did not feel mature enough to handle it.

I finally had the big answers I needed to discover my purpose. I had unlocked the reasons behind my own self-defeating behaviors that I struggled with and that drove me crazy. I knew I had bad behaviors, but felt powerless to change them. I did not know how until I took Life Skills. When I figured out many of the answers and put them to work within myself, I began to see results. I needed to share my discovery with others who had similar struggles. I knew that if I had these struggles in my life, that I surely could not be alone. Others too must have similar struggles as well. Thus, the teacher in me was born. I had never thought myself to be a real teacher, but more of a mentor to others. It was important to me to help others search and find the peace and freedom from bondage that I had discovered for myself. I developed a tremendous passion to share what I had learned with others. I felt an urgent desire to tell others about how God had filled my void, when nothing else could. I now have skills to use as tools to change things that were once out of my control and a Lord that loves me and guides me on the path where He has placed my feet.

Navigating the darkness is something that we all do at some point in our lives. Some experience it more than others and some stay in the darkness longer than others. Some face more intensity than others. While some people, never come out of the dark, as evidenced by extremely high suicide rates and not to mention the tremendous murder rate in America. In Chicago alone, 2016 was considered the "deadliest year in nearly two decades", according to CNN.com dated Jan.2, 2017. Murder rate was up 72% in 2016, while overall shootings were up 88% according to USA Today (4/1/2016). Those stats were just in the first four months of that year! The year was not even over yet. Too much anger and unchecked emotions are exploding. People need help!

Twenty-Two American Veterans a day are killing themselves as told by the Department of Veteran Affairs (DVA). The data collected on the Veterans was during the time of 1999-2010. On average, there are 117 suicides in the generalized American public with 3.5 times more men killing themselves than women according to AFSP.org. According to the New York Times a study showed that we are experiencing "a surge to a 30-year all time high" of American suicides. The article dated April 22, 2016 reports, "In all, 42,773 people died from suicide in 2014, compared with 29,199 in 1999." One suicide is too many.

I feel strongly that those that have navigated the darkness successfully have a duty or even a responsibility to grasp the hands of those that are drowning in a sea of circumstance and guide them out of the darkness of which they are entrapped. We must be navigators, teachers and lovingly point to the light that brings them the hope that they cannot see for themselves. In some cases, we may be the only light in this shadowy world that a person may see. Depression is not an effortless walk alone. It is an uphill battle of unending loneliness in a crowd of people and social isolation. We, that suffer from depression, feel very alone. We believe that no one can possibly understand what we go through daily, yet millions of people suffer with this debilitating illness. We need one another. We need to encourage each other by using our experiences to offer hope where there seemingly is none.

We that have been in a dark state of mind or in a deep-seated depression at some point in our lives, owe it to others to help them out of their depression or difficulties in life. We owe it to ourselves. We know the struggle is real. We have all at some point, wished we had, had someone to help us when no one was there for us. We also know how difficult it is to ask for help. This means that we need to be aware of those around us and watch for the warning signs. We know them. We had them. Take risk and extend a hand of hope. Share your heart and help heal a heart.

Not only do we help others in this process of reaching out and guiding, but we help ourselves by helping others. We gain purpose for our lives, and healing for our souls. We may even leave a legacy when we die, as I will prove to you on Hanover Street when I introduce to you Mr. Mullins and Mr. Owl. Never did they imagine that the time that they spent with a little girl in the 1960's would have led them to having a legacy for themselves that would end up in a book in 2017. We never know who we may influence in life or how we may make a difference in someone's life that could literally include their choice of life or death. Not that we are responsible for the choice of someone who may commit suicide, we are not. We however, can make an enormous difference in their decision-making process by causing them to rethink their decision. We can be a life line that causes them to choose life.

We that have bumped our heads on every imaginable hindrance along the way trying to save ourselves, have basically developed a road map out of situations through trial and error. We must share our knowledge to those in need. Not every person will have the same road maps. We all have lived through different situations in life. We all must network with one another and share our experiences. We can then send people we know that are hurting in specific areas in their lives to those that have had the similar circumstances in their lives. They will have the experiences and wisdom that is needed to assist the hurting person out of the darkness. Local churches are a wonderful place for this type of networking. When we begin this process of networking and helping one another, it begins a building of relationships. People will never care what you know until they know that you care for them. How do we network? Share our testimonies! I love churches that allow a five-minute testimony each week by someone in the congregation.

This allows people to display their road map of experience. This lets people know that there is hope!

Not everyone will accept the help that we offer, but it doesn't mean that we do not try. They may not have hit their rock bottom yet. There will come a time that they will. We all do at some point. We need to be ready to give a hand up when they do. They will know who to come back to for help when it is their time for healing.

I have learned that not every road map will work for every person. This book may help many and sadly there may be many that it won't help. This was an internal conflict within me and prevented me from staying focused and just writing the book. I kept asking, "Who am I" and then I would answer, "Nobody". Then I would say, "Who would ever read a book like this?" then I would answer, "Nobody". I was allowing the negative self-talk to dictate an outcome. I was sabotaging my dreams of helping others.

Realistically I knew that I cannot help everyone. Once I woke up and thought about the goal, which was building the Kingdom for God, it became clear. If you were the only person in the world that needed salvation, Jesus still would have gone to the cross for you. I must emulate my leader. If you were the only person who read this book and it helped you, it was worth every minute of writing it. This book is for you. The point being, you are important and God can and will use you if you will allow Him to.

Dark times come in all shapes, sizes and various lengths of time in our lives. Being unable to write this book when I knew that I should, was a very difficult and conflicting time in my life. I was in that desert again. I was self-sabotaging, and delaying the work of the Lord. I knew that God had called me to do this. I knew that it was an ardent desire within me to do it, but I just did not feel that I was a somebody. Depression can crush confidence. I do not need to be a "somebody" to be helpful to someone. I just need to be me. I need to be humble, caring and empathetic to the needs of others. I need to renounce selfishness. I need to be bold and share my testimony with anyone that will listen and so do you.

I was a teacher of Life Skills which is basically teaching people the reasons behind the behaviors we repetitively do which sabotages our lives. To understand our behaviors, allows us hope for possible change. What we understand, we can change. As a facilitator of Life Skills, I would equip people with coping skills needed to change the malignant and destructive behaviors that had been destroying their lives and all those around them. I would try to encourage them to make a better life for themselves. I gave them a road map. They had to choose to use it, or not. Many did, many did not.

I did not teach as someone that thought themselves to be a wiser and holier-than-thou expert. I taught as a person who has walked their path, felt their pain and through great adversity learned how to emerge from the depths of various hells in my life. My hope was that the student would listen to what I had experienced and identify or connect in some form of understanding. If their situation was like mine, then we could most generally make a solid connection. This offered them hope. They could see someone who had "been there and done that", and made it through. This meant that they could as well. Once a connection was made, the student would try some of the skills I had taught them. Our goal in class was to change the outcome of their situation so that they could eventually emerge as victors and no longer be victims of circumstance.

Another thing I have learned is that each battle that we face is also refining our character and polishing our skills. Each struggle is like a refining fire that burns the dross off the silver. It is a transformation process that is difficult at times, but the emerging result is beautiful and shiny. The battles will never stop coming. The learning and growing will not stop either. We will never know it all on this side of Heaven, but if we are equipped with the right skills and the full armor of God we do not have to suffer in the pits like we have in the past or present.

Another thing I learned while teaching Life Skills is during a "desert moment" I had to stop thinking horizontally and learn to think vertically. This was a huge revelation for me in many aspects of my life, especially now in fighting the enemy against why I should or should not write this book. If only one person should read this book and would receive healing from it, then this book has been worth the battle. The desert time that I have spent learning, has been long. I have struggled most of my life with being stubborn and rebellious. This attributed a great deal of conflict between my mother and myself through the early years. Therefore, if my mom were the only person that read this book, again, it is worth it if she is nothing more than proud of me for the changes I have made in my life. I will explain more about horizontal and vertical thinking later in the book.

When the Lord did not approve of how I had written the book the second time I was crushed. I took it way too personal and I should have. Yes, I said I should have. He was not criticizing me, he was refining me. I was writing it like an instruction book that was too impersonal. He wanted me to be more personal and share with others like I had shared in Life Skills. Life Skills was not successful because of how the facilitators had shared the instructions of skills but rather how they shared their hearts and what they had gone through to get where they were. Then they showed how they applied the skills to make significant changes in their own lives as the example to follow.

The Lord wanted us to use our testimony to make a difference. Why? Because our personal testimonies cannot be disputed because they are personal. If I wrote from the side of a psychology point of view, then every critic in the world would debate and tear apart every word that I wrote. I only recently learned this through simple political debates with people who unfriended me for my thoughts and beliefs. We have no respect for one another's opinions anymore in America. It is sad that we cannot share thoughts without causing war. This book will no doubt still cause controversy and possibly more loss of friends who do not believe as I believe. It is not my will to please them but to please God. I will not debate my testimony. It will either be accepted or rejected. Those that accept it may find some hope to apply to their own lives. Those that reject it are not at a place in their life ready to receive it, but their day will come.

I will be writing each chapter using an excerpt of my life that was a pivotal and sometimes traumatizing time in my life. I will tell the story as my personal testimony, then I will explain how different people entered my life to help me navigate my darkness or how I helped others to navigate their darkness. It is my hope that the Lord will then bring understanding into the heart of the reader of how to apply it to their own lives. I am no expert in psychology even though I have been a psychiatric nurse for over 25 years. I am however an expert on hardship, pain, trauma and heartache. My prayer is that maybe some of what I have experienced will help you to navigate out of your darkness, or your desert, or maybe even teach you to use your own experiences to help navigate others through their hard times.

It is not easy to lay my life bare in front of others to read. I do know that someday we all will have our lives laid bare in front of one another as we are held accountable by the Lord on Judgment day. Transparency now, using my mistakes to help and encourage others, only makes sense. I hope that all the things I may have done to others or what others may have done to me can and will be used to glorify God and that we will all be forgiven through Jesus Christ. As God uses the ashes of my past to make something beautiful for my future, my hope is that it would or could in some way benefit others as well.

Do not be discouraged in your quest to be emotionally healed. It took you many years to get where you are and it will take a little time to rise out of the darkness. There is hope. This I have learned along the way, mountain top experiences are not meant to be long lasting. We all have those moments to stand proud on the mountain top. We look back to see how far we have come and we look ahead to see how much further we must go. The time spent on the mountain top is but a moment to bask in the fact that we have made it this far. Nothing grows above the timber line. It is in the valleys that the rain and sun join forces to sprout the seeds that have been scattered upon good soil to create new and sustaining growth in our lives. Do not hate the valleys, but learn to embrace them. Recognize them for what they are, an incubator of life.

Every valley I now dip into, I immediately ask God, "What do you want me to learn here, Lord?" I want to learn it and learn it quickly if possible. I do not want to wander in the desert for forty years. I continue to waste time even though I have learned the correct way to respond to the valleys. Old habits sometimes rear their ugly heads and I fall. Prepare for the next battle by learning the details of the current battle and move on. For what you have just learned will be the missing puzzle piece to the answers needed in the next battle.

Learn what the Lord is trying to teach you and apply it to your life. Stop being stubborn, prideful and arrogant along the way. I have wasted years of precious life being stubborn and prideful. Don't you. Be obedient to the instruction of the Lord. The Lord has a plan for each one of us (Jeremiah 29:11), if we would only submit to his will and follow his heart. Learn and teach others.

This is our purpose. Go and make disciples of all nations (Matthew 28:16-20). Once you have cared enough to help others, they will possibly care enough to know the God that sent you to help them. No one cares about who our God is, until they have witnessed the power of who He is through those who call themselves a child of God. Do we reflect well who God says He is? Do we bring shame upon the name of the Lord with inappropriate words or actions? Do we cause strife or cause others to stumble in their faith by our poor and incongruent behaviors by not being who we claim to be? If we behave as one person at home and someone different at church, then we have problems. We need to clean up our porch. A double minded person is unstable in all their ways (James 1:8). If we hope to make changes in the lives of others, then we must live the life that we claim to live no matter where we are, whether at home, the store, the church or on Facebook. No one will ever trust or respect a double minded person. They certainly will not take wisdom or suggestions from a person like that either. Though we are not perfect people, we must try to live a life of integrity to the best of our ability.

Love is the answer. Give it freely to others and give the credit to the Lord. Without God blessing us, we cannot bless others. We are the children of the light once we have accepted Christ as our savior. The light that we have ignited within ourselves, through the injection of the Lord Jesus Christ, means that we have taken on the important work of the family business. It is to grow the Kingdom of our Heavenly Father. He is the ultimate light and glory of the world. Let His light shine brightly through us! Though our lights may be sometimes dim through our dark times, together in support of one another we can be a flame that cannot be extinguished.

I have been asked many times throughout my life, "If you could, would you change things in your life?" I used to say the obvious answer, "Absolutely!" Mainly because no one wants to suffer adversity in their lives. However, as I got older and a bit wiser, I realized that it was the adversity which I had suffered that shaped me into the person that I had grown to be. I like who I have become for the most part. Now if asked, I would say, "Absolutely not! I would not change a thing no matter how bad it may have been at times. I am who I am because of what I have been through and because of who God says that I am."

I have gained insight into understanding why people react and behave the way that they do in direct relation to what they have suffered in their own lives. I can forgive inappropriate behaviors almost immediately from the moment it has been committed. I have more empathy for others than I once had. I try to extend the same amount of grace and mercy toward others, as I want to receive for myself from other people and from God. Does this make me perfect? No. It does makes me tolerant of things that I once could not tolerate because He who has done a "good work" in me, is doing a "good work" in others too. It allows me to love those who are difficult to love. I once was very difficult to love and for some people, I still am. It has molded me to become a peace keeper. I try to maintain peace at all cost. However, I do set limits and boundaries using God's word. I will not be run over by people who are only out for themselves. People function from their pain. Knowing this helps us love them despite themselves. I will probably say this again, but the deeper the pain, the higher the expectations we have of self and others. Our expectations will adjust as our pain heals.

We all have choices to make in life. How we react or respond to others is one choice we make daily. God made a choice to turn His wrath into mercy when He sent Jesus to die for us. We can choose to either be bitter and hate filled in our anger, or we can choose to extend mercy. The choice is ours.

I am thankful to the Lord that He has taught me the importance of these character traits and helped guide me through dark times when I could have easily just been consumed by the depression, anxiety and grief instead. God never left my side as I wandered through the darkness and He sent various people into my life to help navigate me when I needed it. There were even a few times when there were not people available to help me and the Lord navigated me Himself. Although I did not recognize it immediately at the time; God was always with me. It became evident once the light began to shine.

Through the grace, love and mercy of my Lord Jesus Christ I have navigated the dark with a heart that was very dimly lit and I emerged victorious as a child of light with a renewed sense of purpose to help others. You can too.

PART ONE

THE TESTIMONIES

CHAPTER 1

FILLING THE VOID

When a person finally hits rock bottom, they are usually at their lowest point in their lives. They are broken in heart, emotions and spirit and physically cannot go on. This is a dangerous place to be in. It is a place where they can either explode outward on others in rage and bitterness or they can implode destroying themselves with rage and self-loathing. To explode means that others will pay for their pain. To implode means the person in emotional pain will pay the debt themselves. The pendulum can be as extreme as the emotions that the person is feeling. The pendulum swing of extreme could swing from homicide to suicide or land anywhere in between. The extreme of the extreme would be someone that wanted others to pay and then take on the pain themselves as well. This would be a homicide/suicide situation. Very devastating to families left picking up the pieces when this happens.

In the twenty plus years that I have had the honor of teaching those who have hit rock bottom in a formal program setting, I have learned to ask questions. I wanted to know: what the person was feeling, if they even knew how to feel, did they have a feeling of purpose in life and what did they feel was missing in their lives? And though I have received numerous answers throughout the years there is a consensus response that I feel is important to address. I too felt this way at my rock bottom. The answers given were:

1. They do not know what they feel.
2. They do not know how to feel.
3. They do not recognize emotions and cannot name them when they do feel them. There are three emotions that nearly everyone could identify, which was happy, sad and mad.
4. They do not know how to handle the emotions and so the emotions dominate them.
5. They do not love or even like themselves.
6. They do not feel that their lives are important.
7. They feel that their lives lack purpose, meaning and direction.
8. They feel that the people they love would be better off without them.
9. They feel total rejection without knowing why, even when they have strong supportive families.
10. They feel like failures and are embarrassed by their behaviors but feel powerless to stop or change them.
11. They feel empty and unloved.
12. They believe that something is missing in their lives and they do not know what it is nor how to find it.
13. Of those that identified that they lacked a spiritual aspect to their lives, which most identified as God, they did not feel worthy to even approach Him to ask for help. Many were either embarrassed or felt too much shame to even consider asking Him. Of the people that claimed to be atheist or agnostic, through the course of the program it was discovered that most did believe in God, but were angry at him for not responding to their needs. I discovered, the people with misdirected anger, many of them had spiritual immaturity that seemed to match or coincide with their emotional developmental age.

In the nursing field in the1980's we were trained that holistic nursing was important to help our patient heal within their mind, body and spirit. It was considered important for the overall health of the person, but became taboo when it came time to enter a work force. We were threatened that we could not talk about the spiritual side because we may offend someone, cause a law suit or overstep our bounds due to our own beliefs. It was politically incorrect. We certainly were not allowed to proselytize at all, that was a "no, no!" So how do we help heal the person holistically with such boundaries? How do we help the person fill the void that they have? By being politically correct of course with psychotherapy and medications only. It was and is the culture of our times. However, those two things do not always fill the void the person is struggling with and we should offer more. Individualized care is a must!

There comes a time that you must learn to also navigate the darkness of politics the best that you can. When a person is, down and lacking the "light" they are seeking so desperately to find, I simply ask them a question. In assessments, we must ask questions to get to the root cause of the problem to help the person appropriately. Nurses are much like investigators in that we must ask questions and probe deeper depending on the responses that we receive. One of the questions I ask is, "Are you a person of faith? It is a simple question and has always opened a door to allow for follow up questions such as: Has it failed you? What does your faith tell you in this type situation?" Their responses are good indicators of how they were raised and what they were taught to believe or not believe. People will live by their life commandments and some will die by them. Life commandments are their belief systems.

Even if I was not wanting to help fill their void with God (which I do), I would need to know this information because what a person believes can cure them or kill them. Our minds are capable of believing anything, fact or fiction. If our beliefs are strong enough to cause anxiety and stress, then over time, it can and will erode the body systems and can in extreme cases cause possible psychosomatic death.

Case and point. I have raised my two oldest granddaughters for most of their lives. Their parents were young and needed help. With the help of the maternal grandmother, she and I together became a significant part of these girls' lives. For purposes of privacy I will call the maternal grandmother Sandy. Sandy had many heart aches in her life for most of her life but was a wonderful grandmother. Our granddaughters brought so much joy to both of us that we could not imagine not having them in our lives. Sandy was disabled and due to her disability, it allowed her to babysit for me when I had to work which was ideal in this situation. We did not have to rely on outsiders to babysit and it kept balance in the lives of our granddaughters. It worked out well for everyone involved including the parents that were very involved in their lives as well.

The reason Sandy was disabled was because she had numerous illnesses that kept her from living a normal daily life. She had to go to the doctor's office a lot for various symptoms and problems. She ended up on numerous medications. They would treat her symptoms that they did not have a definitive answer for or diagnosis. Her dependency on the drugs became more and more evident as the weeks, months, and years passed. Her illness became worse and there were no answers. She went to many specialists and no one had an answer but kept giving her drugs to treat the symptoms of an unknown illness. We all were very concerned for her and prayed for her a lot.

In the wee hours of April 4, 2010 I received a frantic call from my son crying and telling me that Sandy was dead! I raised up in the bed and screamed, "What do you mean she is dead? How? Why? What happened?" My son did not have answers other than she was found having a seizure and they ambulanced her to the hospital where she went into cardiac arrest and could not be revived. This was devastating news for everyone! The impact it created on this family and her immediate family was of great magnitude. She was loved, she was needed and she was only 43 years old. How could this happen?

Sandy's oldest daughter, (mother of our granddaughters) was relentless trying to find out the reason or cause of her death. The coroner was excellent in wanting to find out, why someone so young, would die so soon with no real reason to do so. We as a family had been told by Sandy that she had muscular sclerosis. Later, she revealed that "they" thought it might be a brain tumor, but it had not yet been an absolute diagnosis. Considering the seizure, she had suffered, we thought that it was a good possibility. We had no reason to doubt what she was saying might not be true. However, what we discovered by her autopsy was this; there was no reason this 43-year-old woman should have died. Basically, it appears she died a psycho-somatic death, but it was never confirmed. It is a death that she may have created by the worry and the belief that she was sick. She may not have been physically sick primarily, it may have been secondary to the belief she had in her mind that she was sick and that she was dying. Her mind may have convinced her body that she was sick and dying. She was not dying initially, but over time her mind created the outcome and she eventually did die. Mental illness comes in many forms and this is one possible type. A tremendous loss for our families!

Since our brains can believe anything, she may have trained her brain to believe the darkest of all things. Her brain then responded to the belief that she had instilled upon her own subconscious mind. She buried her emotional pain so deeply, that she would not, or could not deal with it. It was too painful. So, she focused on the physical pain that she could medicate herself to obtain relief. Many people self-medicate and they get into a vicious cycle that they cannot pull themselves up and out of. Interestingly, her toxicology screens were negative. No signs of an overdose of any drug. No signs of the illnesses that she claimed to have. No logical reason to have died.

The medications did not heal her emotional pain and though there were times I tried to reach out to her emotionally she would dismiss it and change the subject. We had a close friendship but she simply did not allow anyone to enter her pain because she was not able to enter it herself. She would talk of God a little bit but she would not go deep into it. I would invite her to church and she came some but the pain of her emotional wounds would not allow her to even approach God at times. She eventually quit church as well. However, I still believe that God was all that she clung to right up until the end.

This death changed everything, every situation and every person in the family to some degree. I felt like a failure because I didn't push harder to help her. I had done all that I was permitted to do. I had invited her to take the classes I taught, I gave her books on the classes I taught. She was not receptive. Her pain was simply too deep and it had been let go like an undiagnosed cancer for way too long. She was a deeply depressed person and her only ability to survive was to focus on symptoms and treat them as they arose. This was a tragic loss and there was no one to navigate her darkness. Sandy's darkness rocked her to her very core.

We must know what is causing a person to be on rock bottom and we must explore every avenue of the mind, body and spirit. A tri-pod can maintain balance. A two-legged chair cannot be balanced. As psychiatric nurses, we were made to try and teach our patients to balance that which could not balance. We would stabilize people on two legs and send them home to do a balancing act, but the two-legged chair would eventually fall. The patient would be back another day to be readmitted. Not everyone will accept the God as I know him. I realize that. But that does not mean that we should not address their spiritual side of their lives. Everyone has a spiritual side or holistic nursing would have never based a balanced sense of nursing on the mind, body and spirit as we were taught.

So, to fill a void, what do we do?

1. **Investigate, assess and evaluate.** We must ask as many questions as it takes. Do not just scratch the surface. Dig for the root cause. Which means, we ask questions about the answers we have already received from the person. An exhaustive investigation is important as we are fighting for the very lives of people at times. Is asking them questions about their faith politically correct? No! But who cares when you are trying to save their life? If someone was literally drowning in deep ocean water and you happened by in a boat, do you ask them if you can throw them a life preserver or do you just do it and hope they grab it? We save them first and can face criticism later for our lack of political correctness. If a person at rock bottom does not want to discuss God or their faith they will let you know. If they refuse, then you stop. However, I have found that in my many years of nursing and investigating, that the person usually wants to

explore that gaping hole in their heart because it brings a hope that they have lost. The Bible says, "hope deferred makes the heart sick, but when the desire comes, it is a tree of life" (Proverbs 13:12) We must be beacons of light to navigate the dark and bring hope where there is none. Search their heart, mind and soul and learn where the void is and why. Investigate, investigate and investigate some more. Do not fear asking and being very direct with the person. They need it right now.

2. **Establish a relationship.** Define the role you will play. Lay the ground rules and boundaries so that they are clear. Do not take on more than the person is willing to take on for themselves. They must be invested. Yes, we carry them in the beginning of their crisis but it will not take long to establish whether they are invested to help themselves or not. If they are not, then you back away some and let them know that you will enforce the boundaries and will only match their effort. When they have hit their rock bottom then they know how to find you for help. If they are serious about getting help they will return. If they are not, they will continue to do it their way until they are sick and tired of being sick and tired. We cannot enable inappropriate behavior and we cannot force them to accept help they are not ready to receive. Match their efforts. Do not do more than they do. You can lead them to the water but you cannot make them drink. You are not a failure if they choose not to drink. They simply are not ready.
3. **Pray for them** and with them if they will allow it. Simply ask them, "Do you mind, if I say a prayer for you". You will rarely be turned down. A meaningful prayer spoken out loud where they can hear it can do some amazing things.

Remember that they do not feel worthy to approach the throne and so they may run from it and just as Adam hid from God in the garden; so they too hide from God. Remind them of the value that God has placed in them as you pray on their behalf. It will baffle their minds if you speak God's words about who they are in Christ Jesus as you pray for their restoration and healing. It will offer them hope indirectly. The truth will set them free!

4. Help them build an **Action Plan**. We need to take the information we have discovered and begin to offer as many resources as we can. They often feel hopeless and helpless. Show them how to control the controllable. It will empower them to take some control back over their lives. Yes, the situation may be out of their control, but some of the sub-situations may not be. Be an objective viewer and give words of hope. It will help them navigate the maze of self-destruction and show them how to prioritize a way out. Their handling the small stuff and us teaching them to leave the big stuff up to God is important. If that door way has been opened for us to enter, it will make a significant difference in their life. If the spiritual door has not been opened, then just focus on the things that they can do and tell them to leave the rest alone to fix itself because it will. Make sure that the action plan reflects answers and possibilities for **emotional support, physical support and spiritual support**. All 3-topics need addressed.
5. **Resources** such as church support, support groups, networking, and organizations for each of those pillars we discussed must be given to the person so they have a balanced tri-pod. These should be incorporated into the action plan as much as possible.

6. **Identify their strengths.** Their greatest resource is their own talents and strengths. They will not believe that they have any, but we know that is not true. Through investigating and asking questions we can discover some of their own assets and then put them to use. Then we praise them for the ability to do more than they had realized that they were able to do. We embolden them to step up to the plate to do more.
7. **Identify their purpose.** No person has a will to live if their perceived purpose for living is gone. The problem is that most people do not believe that they have a purpose. We identified earlier that if their belief system is stronger than the actual truth it can cause death by either psycho-somatic means or by the hands of the person themselves in extreme cases. We must show them the truth. We must show them their purpose and reason for living. We only open the door to the possibilities, they must push the door on open, should they decide to do so. But we must invoke curiosity so that they want to use the strength it takes to open the door and see what lies behind it. It is human nature to be needed and wanted. It is human nature to want to help others. It is human nature to feel good about ourselves when we do help others and it is human nature to become depressed and give up when we feel we serve no purpose to anyone or anything. We need a cause to rise for and to know that we are helping others in the process. Therefore, I tell people the same thing that was told to me by my mentor, Dr. Paul Hegstrom, Founder of Life Skills International, he said, **"Where your pain is, so therein lies your mission and purpose."** For 12 years, I lived with domestic violence. When I was helped from my hole and realized I had experience and

wisdom to help others, I created a mission to help victims and perpetrators. We all need a purpose. We need a reason to get out of bed.

8. **Where possible, encourage their growth in God.** Sometimes this is not something a person working for a business is able to openly do, but there are ways to do it without breaking rules. Be creative. Know the policy of your organization and work around them the best you can. Many organizations will allow you to speak of spiritual issues if the person/patient brings it up first. If you are however, a mentor with no organization to be accountable to, then be bold and be strong in how you help them to lean on the Lord. Teach them the fundamental basics and put them on a path that will cause them to grow and learn. Do not just lead them to the Lord then drop them, to figure it out on their own. That is spreading seed that will not take root. We must nurture and tend the seed until it is strong enough to sustain itself by a root system. Build this into their action plan. Remember that God is NOT about religion. He is about LOVE. We are pushing relationship, not religion. We are spreading the seeds of love.
9. **Teach them about Responsibility and Accountability.** Be their accountability partner or set them up with one. Jesus mentored his disciples for three years before He left them on their own to go and make disciples of all nations. And even then, He did not leave them completely alone. He sent to them the Holy Spirit to be their counselor who guided them as the Lord wanted them to go.

In section two, I will go more into some of the actual skills that will help you with following these steps. I will show you how to build an action plan using a scenario situation. We must help give people the basics and as many words of wisdom and encouragement as we can. Speak words that are significant and breathe life. Carefully chosen words will stick in their minds. We should mentor just as Jesus did the Apostles. He gave his time freely and was committed to teaching them all that He could, so that they would be successful in the battles that lie ahead of them.

Every battle we face is only preparing us for the next battle that is ahead of us as I have already said and will repeat it again. If we do not learn what God wants us to learn in a specific battle, we will repeat the battle until we do learn. God will not advance our purpose or send us into a battle that we are not ready to face. Though sometimes it feels as though He has. He will never place on us more than He knows we can bear. He will provide for us a means to succeed and a way out of sin and making wrong decisions. We simply must be listening to Him and know His voice and ultimately make the right choice. His sheep will know his voice. Those who do not yet know His voice, needs a mentor who does. A beacon of light in a dark place reduces the fear that we are facing.

CHAPTER 2

HANOVER STREET

As a little girl we lived in Aurora, Colorado. The first home I recall was on Joliet Street where I lived with both my mother and father. My parents managed the Joliet Apartments that my aunt and uncle owned and my dad owned a book store in downtown Denver that he worked at every day.

There are many stories I could tell about this time of my life that were funny and exciting and it would explain to you the type of child I was born to be. I was a strong-willed, headstrong and very adventurous little girl. These stories helped to shape who I was, but they do not reflect darkness in my memories. In fact, these were the sweetest memories that I harbor in my mind, for my family was complete and I felt safe and secure. These times will forever be special times in my heart, but they were not to last and sadly they did not.

Our family was growing as we lived in the apartments and my parents knew we needed more space. At that time living in the apartment we had Mom, Dad, my brother Les, my sister Ruth and myself. Mom was pregnant with twins. It was time to move and move we did. We moved to a house that appeared to look like a mansion to me on Hanover Street. It was amazing coming from the apartment we had lived in the first five years of my life. It was a five-bedroom house with a basement and big fenced in yard.

Believe me, a fence was a good thing when raising me because I was an explorer! Dora had nothing on me back then.

My parents seemed to not get along very well after moving there, but they tried to hide it. I was an observant child and it caused an unsettling inside my heart. It took away the sense of security that I had been so blessed to have had for the first five years of my life.

Soon the twins arrived and we had a new baby girl and baby boy. We could not believe how blessed we were to have not one but two babies in our home. I wanted to help Mom all the time with them and sometimes she would let me. Sometimes I would be re-directed because I wanted to do too much, like when I pulled the umbilical cord off the stomach of my new baby sister. It just looked like it didn't belong there, after all it didn't look like mine. So, I pulled it off. Yes, she cried and later, so did I as mom admonished me and rightfully so.

Mom had five children now all within a five-year span and certainly had her hands full. She loved each one of us and worked so very hard to care for us. There was no doubt that we were loved and loved much. We were more than a hand full. I alone was a handful and usually was the leader of the pack that led to trouble now and again. My great grandmother Dorothy, whom we called Bobo, came to live with us to help Mom with the kids. She was a blessing and we loved her so much. Having her there only made our days brighter.

Dad continued to work long hours at the bookstore and it seemed we saw him less and less each day. Mom seemed less happy and spent more and more time in her room. As the adult influences seemed to be retreating away from our presence, the more my siblings and I became self-reliant and mischievous. Eventually the reality of what was slowly happening in our home became known as Mom and Dad separated and eventually divorced. Not only did we lose our Dad from the house, we then lost Bobo too because that was Dad's grandmother. She went to live with Dad's mom, my grandmother. This was the first time that I recall having such great pain in my life that did not seem to ever want to end. What I learned during this time that was not evident then, but only later as an adult became clear to me, was that children are not afforded the opportunity to grieve and share their feelings in times such as these. We certainly did not have a vote in what was happening to our lives. We were helpless against the decisions of these adults who were so caught up in their own pain and grief that they did not recognize the pain in their children. I have been guilty of the same thing with my own children.

Mom was left to care for us alone for a short while. She was very depressed and sad. Robotically she took care of us the best that she could. She began to go out and have a new life of meeting people and having fun. Her best friend from high school moved in and lived as a nanny, though that was not her primary reason for being there, I do not believe. My mother was a very compassionate person and she would take in anyone who needed help. Linda my mom's friend was very kind. She was a significant role model in our lives and she remained so until the day she died many years later.

Mom met a woman that decided to start a band. Mom at that time could only play the piano, but they needed a bass guitarist. Mom was willing to learn and so she bought a bass guitar and pulled out her Beatles Albums and began to teach herself how to play the bass. Before long they added other members to their band and they began to have band practice at our house. Music permeated the home all the time. For me this was so much better than the doom and gloom we had been facing for a while. We sang and danced around when they practiced. It was a very enjoyable time. It seemed that maybe some happiness was returning to our home, but it was not to last long.

This woman moved in and the band began to work in Idaho Springs, Colorado. They played there every weekend for five years. This was how Mom earned a living to care for her five children. It was not a comfortable or easy living. It was difficult, as anyone who played in a band would know. I recall times when Mom did not have a babysitter for us and would have to take us to work with her. We would sit in a booth by the stage eating maraschino cherries and drinking cokes listening to Mom play and sing her songs until we could not stay awake. Sometimes we would get lucky if it was not too busy and we could dance by the stage until we wore ourselves out. When we were ready for bed, Mom would put us down in the back of the station wagon and laid us on bed pallets she made for us in the far back with seats down. She backed the car up to the side door by the stage and the side door was left open so she could keep an eye on us. Of course, this was in pleasant weather times and did not happen often. She worked hard and she played hard. It was the late 1960s early 70s. Alcohol and drugs entered the scene for both Mom and my dad. We didn't see Dad much anymore and the more the parties grew, the less we saw of Mom as well.

The more time we had on our own with less supervision, the more time we had for our imaginations to go to work. We kids would wander out of our yard and go here and there without letting Mom know. Sometimes we left and got back without her even knowing we were gone. Sometimes we went short distances and sometimes a bit longer distances but we tried to stay within ear shot in case we were called home by Mom's two finger whistle. Man was it loud!

Sometimes the Lord puts people in our paths like guardian angels to protect us and sometimes to teach us life lessons. It was during this time, when Mom lost her way and Dad disappeared, that God did just that for me and my dear siblings.

Enter in, two of the most amazing men in my life that helped to secure up a crumbling shore line in the lives of me and my siblings. Though they most likely never knew it, they were the hands, feet and watchful eye of Jesus as they gave us their time, effort, love and care just by being willing to not shoo us away, but engaged with us in real and tangible ways. They did not know each other but they both literally did the same thing at the same time at opposite ends of the block of Hanover Street. These men's homes became our boundary area. Because of them we did not want to wander any further than the corner of 17th and Hanover and the corner of 18th and Hanover. Mr. Mullins lived on the 17th end of the block and Mr. Owl (who got his name due to his eyebrows and we never knew his real name) lived on the opposite end of the block on 18th Street and Hanover.

Each man had their own purpose in our lives. Sometimes I do not know all that they did to affect my life until I get into a situation where something that they said or did comes back to the forefront of my mind in just the right timing. They were guiding me through the darkness from years ago. Both men have long passed away but their lights still shine bright in the mind and heart of who I am. Their words and deeds that helped to shape who I am are a legacy and testament of who they were as godly men. I thank God for the presence of them during such a dark time in my life.

Mr. Mullins lived right next door to me. He had the biggest yard I had ever seen and it had a hill that we kids could lay down on and roll down until we were so dizzy we could not stand up.

We would climb our fence and get into his yard and play when he was not around. He had a most wonderful garden that he tended to daily that ran along our fence line. One day I decided that I wanted some of what he had in his garden and like any good thief I did not want to go alone. So, I enlisted the help of Les and Ruth, my brother and sister. We climbed over the fence and went straight to the garden to begin pilfering through his garden for good things to eat. This was my first experience with rhubarb. Long slender sticks of a tangy sweet and sour taste that only kept us coming back for more. We would break them off and eat what we could there and then take a handful home with us and eat until our bellies hurt. We always slipped in and out without being caught by Mom or by Mr. Mullins. So, we thought.

One day I heard my mom call for me and my siblings to come to the front door. There in the doorway outside on our porch was our neighbor Mr. Mullins. My heart sank as I just knew he was telling my mom that we had stolen his rhubarb and we were about to get a butt whooping we very much deserved. I was so scared because I knew I deserved it but I didn't want it. Mom started out by saying, "This is Mr. Mullins. He is our neighbor." I thought to myself, "Yep, this is it. He told her and we are dead." I am not sure why I thought that because my mother rarely spanked us. I must have felt conviction.

She then told us that Mr. Mullins had seen that we had been in his garden and that we seemed to really love his rhubarb a lot! I was thinking, "He got that right!" However, I knew that the boom was about to be lowered and not only was the whooping coming but the end of our rhubarb supplier source. A sad day for sure! But something amazing happened when out from behind his back he held out a big ol' pie! Mr. Mullins said, "I figured since you kids loved my rhubarb so much I had my wife make a rhubarb pie to try and we hope you like it." My heart sunk. Guilt overwhelmed me.

Here I had sneaked into this man's garden and stole his rhubarb and ate it in his garden and took extra home knowing it was wrong. I did know right from wrong, mind you. And yet, instead of being angry and hateful about these dang kids destroying his garden he actually made us a pie! He wanted us to eat more!! How could this be? He never complained once to Mom and in fact told her that he did not want us to be in trouble as she apologized for our behavior. I was relieved but shocked all at the same time. I already loved this man!

He said that he did not mind that we ate from his garden but preferred we picked the fruit of it with him so that we did not pick the wrong things or harm the growth of his plants so that we could eventually have more. He wanted to teach us a little bit about gardening if we wanted to learn. I was so excited and I asked if I could go over there with him. Mom said yes, that we could go. This began the mentorship, relationship, guidance and counsellorship of Mr. Mullins in my life. This is also where I first learned what it meant to be shown grace and mercy for bad behaviors when it was not deserved. Though I didn't recognize it for what it was then, I learned to put that puzzle piece into significant spots in my adult life when the time came. That man planted more than rhubarb seeds into the ground that day. He planted seeds inside of me and though when it was time for the harvest of what he had planted in me to come, he was not alive to see it, but the Lord did and will credit Mr. Mullins for it.

Mr. Mullins asked me as we worked in his garden if I knew who Jesus was? I kinda did I told him because Mom had taken us to church sometimes. He asked if I wanted to go to church with him on Sunday and I told him that I did. You see, he built a relationship with me in the rhubarb garden and he showed me that he truly cared. Because he cared about me, I cared about him. What he cared about, I began to care about. I wanted to make him happy like he had made me happy.

I asked mom if I could go to church with Mr. Mullins and she said I could go. On Sunday morning, rather than jumping his fence as I always had done, I went around the fence that separated our homes by using the sidewalk and used his gate to enter his yard. I rang his door bell and he answered the door with a great big smile and said, "You ready to go?" I said I was and he stepped outside and he said that we were going to walk to church because it was a beautiful day. And that it was.

He walked with a cane and so we walked rather slowly. He would hold my hand because I was about six years old and we had some busy streets to cross to get to the church. It was a big white Baptist church on Havana Street not too many blocks from our houses. This became a ritual each Sunday that we would walk to and from Church together. When we got back from church, we would sit on his porch and I would pick the small stones from the tread of his cane. We talked about what we had learned at church that Sunday and about how much Jesus loved me.

My imagination would paint the pictures in my mind as he would talk to me about Jesus and he made Jesus come alive to me even though I could not see him literally. Later when Mr. Mullins took ill and then had to go to a nursing home he made sure that someone from that church continued to come and get me and take me to church. I continued for a while but life would change things. Seeds were planted in me by a most wonderful man whom I will always love and cherish in my heart and mind. I missed him so much when he left and was very sad for my loss of a great friend.

Now as you may recall, I said that there were two men simultaneously guarding the borders of Hanover Street. Allow me to introduce you to my other guardian angel, Mr. Owl at the other end of the street. When Mr. Mullins was busy or not home then I would get my wandering shoes on and veer out in search of something to do. Usually it wasn't good but I did not mean it to be that way, it just turned out that way. In trying to expand my borders I decided to go down the other way from Mr. Mullins house and explore that direction. As I got to the end of the street there was a man outside with some tables set up and on the tables, were tons of beautiful plants. Some were the most colorful plants I had ever seen. I stopped at his gate and just stood there watching him and didn't say a word. I just wanted to see what he was up to.

He was an old man as well and he had these great big bushy eyebrows and they were perfectly in place as they turned up at the ends of his eyes making him look like an owl. He had a pipe in his mouth as he worked and the smell from that pipe was the sweetest smell I think I had ever smelled coming from smoke. I liked it a lot. He continued to busy himself, doing as he was before I had arrived and really didn't acknowledge me right off the bat. I had seen that he noticed I was there but he did not appear to be that friendly. That was no matter to me. I am a pretty stubborn person and nosey sometimes as well. I was determined to find out what he was doing.

I continued to just stand and watch his every move as he seemed to be planting and repotting plants though I did not understand what he was doing at that time. When he saw my persistence of not leaving, he finally asked me what I was doing? I said that I was watching him doing what he was doing. He wanted to know if I knew what he was doing and I said that no I did not. He then wanted to know if I was interested in what he was doing and I said that I was. All the while wondering why he would ask that because obviously, I was standing there watching him. He hadn't invited me into the gate and I had been taught we don't enter without invitation. Yes, I know that didn't work so well with Mr. Mullins' garden. However, Mr. Owl was standing right there and I dare not come in without an invitation. He didn't seem to want to ask me to come in. So, what is a girl to do? I invited myself to come on in! "Can I come in and see what you are doing?" He turned and with a very little smirk, he smiled and said, "Yes, I thought you'd never ask."

I opened the gate and he reminded me to make sure I closed it behind me, which I did. I ran up the sidewalk to where he was working and I began asking tons of questions. I asked what he was doing and why he was doing it. I asked his name though he did not readily tell me at first. I asked about his pipe and what the smell was that came from it. Oh, I am very sure that he was truly regretting having allowed me to invite myself into his yard due to all the questions I was asking. He lived in a great big house that was much like ours and he lived all alone. He was a very private man and I never did learn much about him. I do know however that he didn't totally live alone. He had a very teeny tiny man that lived with him and his name was Mr. Abercrombie. I will tell you more about him in a minute.

Our first meeting did not get off the ground too well, but he did show me what he was doing. He explained, sometimes when plants outgrow their pots, they must move into something bigger. So, he was giving the plants that had outgrown their old homes a new home which was the bigger pot that he was placing them in. I understood that analogy because our family had outgrown our house and we had to move and get a new one too. He taught me that sometimes when leaves start to die that they should be removed because they suck the energy away from the rest of the plant and it puts the whole plant in danger of dying. By removing or pruning the dead leaves it not only preserves the life of the plant and it gives energy for it to grow even bigger. It will produce other baby plants that he can later separate and grow in different pots. I was eager to learn what he was doing and loved listening to him explain why he did what he did. He asked if I liked his plants and I said I loved them! They were beautiful!

He laughed then said, "Come inside with me then." I know what you're thinking. How dangerous this whole scenario was and how bad it could have been, especially currently when children come up missing all the time. The Lord's hand was all over this and safe I was, thanks to the Lord. I entered the house with him and he took me into his dining room and it was full wall to wall with plants galore! He had them under purple lighting and they were colorful and of all sizes and shapes. My eyes could not believe what I was seeing. They were beautiful and I wanted one!

Time seemed to be flying by and I knew I needed to get home. I told him I had to get home now. He asked me if I would like a plant to take home and I was so excited and said, "Yes!" He told me to pick one and I picked out one that was big and colorful and he told me it was a Coleus plant and he told me just how to care for it. He told me that it can be fragile and it was up to me to keep it alive and he would count on me to do it and not let him down. I promised I would. I asked if I could come back and he said I could, but I don't think he expected me to come every day like I initially did. He had to finally set a limit and I went down there on Saturday mornings. It was great. Saturday with Mr. Owl and Sunday with Mr. Mullins.

I took my plant and thanked him and headed home. When I got home and told Mom about my great adventure she asked where I got the plant and I told her Mr. Owl gave it to me. I told her all about him and how he taught me to care for this plant. She told me I should not accept gifts from strangers and that I should take it back to him. I was crushed. I slowly walked back to his house with the plant and he was back outside finishing up his potting process. He asked why I was so sad. I told him that Mom said that I could not take gifts from strangers. He thought a moment and then said to come inside. I followed him inside. We sat down in his living room and he sat back into his chair. He grabbed a pouch and pulled out some black looking stuff that I had never seen and he put it into his pipe. He then took a metal thing and tapped it down into the pipe. He never said a word this whole time. I just sat there in awe watching what he was doing filled with great anticipation for what he was about to do.

He lit the pipe with a zippo lighter and began to puff and puff on that pipe. He held two fingers over the top of the tobacco area and would move them up and down as he sucked on the pipe as the pipe began to get hotter and hotter it began to make a noise. Not a noise that was accidental but it was very much on purpose. The noise almost sounded like someone was talking in a squeaky voice but I could not make out the words. I began to laugh and he smiled slightly and winked with those bushy eyes and said, "I want to introduce you to Mr. Abercrombie. He lives with me here in this house. I am Mr. Owl, which is why my eye brows look as they do." I wondered if he was a real owl or not but I dared not ask. But I did ask him who Mr. Abercrombie was? He simply stated that he was a little man who lived in his pipe and he kept him company on days that he would get lonely. That was it! I had two new friends and we no longer were strangers which was the point that Mr. Owl was trying to make. I did believe that I now had two new friends. I knew that I was lonely sometimes, but I didn't have to be anymore between Mr. Mullins, Mr. Owl and Mr. Abercrombie. How could I ever be lonely again?! Life was good again.

I got to where I could not wait to go and visit both Mr. Owl and Mr. Abercrombie. Mr. Owl would have to translate the stories that Mr. Abercrombie would tell because I could not really understand him very well. The stories were amazing and always kept my imagination pumped. I wanted to hear more and more, but Mr. Owl would get tired easily and he would send me on my way so that he could lay down and take a nap.

On the day, he introduced me to Mr. Abercrombie he stood up when it was time for me to go and went into the dining room and gave me a second plant and told me to take both plants home. One was for me which I still had in my hand and the other was for my mother. We were friends now and not strangers he said. I ran home and told Mom. With hesitation, she accepted the plant. She went to meet him at some point and after that I got to go down there a lot to see him but mostly on Saturdays.

I believe that I really don't have to tell you all that Mr. Owl taught me here. Just like Mr. Mullins, he had a purpose in my life and what I find totally amazing is that both men or should I say all three of these men not only played a significant role in my life but they were in sync to what they were each teaching me. They both were teaching me the principles of sowing and reaping, grace and mercy, relationship and love. They both molded my life with gentleness and kindness which they never had to do, but did. They could have been crotchety old men and told me to go away, but they didn't. They were a light in my newly dimming world. They were teaching me foundational biblical truths that would someday make more sense to me. They helped to shape my character to become who I am today.

Sometimes we do not realize the significance of our daily interactions with other people. We dismiss the importance of what a kind word or ten minutes of our time could mean to someone. What would have happened to this little girl if there were not two men at either end of the street of which I lived that provided an unspoken boundary for me? With my adventurous spirit, back then I would have roamed much further and could have been lost forever or worse yet been kidnapped or killed. The Lord provided a need through two-and-a-half men that without them I would have been lonely and lost in the darkness. They provided the light that I needed to grow, they pruned the deadness inside me and encouraged life. They instilled hope when I had none and something to look forward to each day I woke up. I would get my brother and sister to tag along with me from time to time and I believe that they loved them too.

Mr. Owl's health deteriorated as did Mr. Mullins' health. One day I went to Mr. Owls' house and he was packing. I was devastated. I asked where he was going and he would not tell me. He said it was better that I not know but that I did need to know that he cared about me and would miss me very much. I could not understand why he would not tell me, but when I got older and thought back I figured he was going to a nursing home or worse. I thought it must have been something bad happening and that is why he would not tell me. He didn't want me to hurt. He gave me more plants and told me to take diligent care of them and as long as I had them with me, I had him with me. I remember crying a lot that day. He made me leave. I think because he was going to cry too and was not going to do it in front of me. I remember thinking years later that he must have been terminally ill and just could not bring himself to tell me that.

Can you imagine if we emulated every positive interaction that we have had with positive people in our lives and replicated it in the lives of others what our world would be like? Many people that know me, know Mr. Mullins and Mr. Owl in a real and personal way. Because how they treated me is how I try to treat others and had they not treated me that way I would not be who I am today. Their legacy lives on past the lives they lived and died with. The word of God that Mr. Mullins planted in me grew with the help of Mr. Owl. Though he did not talk about Jesus to me, he did bear witness to every word that Mr. Mullins spoke to me and planted inside my heart. Coincidence? I think not. I think it was a divine appointment from God that both men took the time and effort to accept the assignment of a pesky six-year-old girl and they made a difference. They lit the path of the road map and showed me a way out of the darkness.

As I said earlier, each battle we face prepares us for the next battle that lies ahead. Little did I know that not long after these two wonderful men that were in my life had to leave, that I too would be leaving Hanover Street for a time. I would be placed into foster care. The next battle begins. However, I do not go alone. I carry with me Mr. Mullins, Mr. Owl and Mr. Abercrombie and an honorable mention of Mrs. Palmer, my Kindergarten teacher. She loved me so much and equaled or even surpassed the love of these men I wrote about here.

The Lord never leaves us in times of need, but he does prepare us to handle whatever battle we may face, which makes God there in our midst to face the journey ahead.

RECAP OF WHAT I LEARNED:

1. Love a stranger
2. Don't steal from your neighbor or covet what he has
3. Extend grace and mercy in the measure that you would want to receive it
4. Listen and learn, apply what you learn
5. Use your imagination
6. Take care of that which is weaker and dependent upon others to live
7. Build relationships to make a person porous that they may absorb your love and words that you plant in their hearts and minds
8. You always reap what you sow.

RECAP OF CHARACTER TRAITS THAT WERE BEING FORMED IN ME:

1. Compassion
2. Truthfulness
3. Honesty
4. Integrity,
5. Respectfulness
6. A sense of boundaries and limitation
7. Mercy, Grace, Loving forgiveness
8. Empathy and love.

I am not bragging. These traits did not emerge fully grown inside of me. They were the seeds that were planted in my heart and through the years with them being watered, tended and grown in the valleys of which I have walked, they began to grow and develop in my life.

Seeds come from full grown fruit. Mr. Mullins and Mr. Owl could not plant seeds inside of me that they themselves did not possess for themselves. It is impossible to give what you do not have. I am thankful for the seeds that they gave to me. Their lights were bright and illuminated a dark and scary time of uncertainty in my life. I did not recognize at that age in my life just what a significant part they played in protecting me, teaching me, guiding me and shaping my future. My parents also planted many seeds that were good, for which I am thankful.

CHAPTER 3

MY TROUBLED TEENS

As I look back through my life considering which parts I should share, it became very evident to me that God was with me every step of the way. He was there through the times that I very much felt alone and abandoned. For this very reason, it has made it very hard to pick out a few among the many testimonies of my life to share with you.

My teen years were extremely turbulent and difficult for me. Teenagers have a very difficult time under normal circumstances growing with hormonal changes and discovering who they are as an individual. When you throw in total dysfunction and chaos then that is like throwing fuel on a fire. It is an explosive and sometimes implosive situation. This was my situation. I cannot share every step of my teens due to time constraints but I want to share the darkest times of those years to show that Jesus held my hand and protected me through every step of the way and sometimes it was just Him and me. Other times he would send in someone to be my beacon of light to navigate me through the storm.

After coming out of the foster home at around age eight, I went to live with my grandparents for a while. Eventually we could move back home with our mother to Hanover Street. As life continued with various struggles related to our home life, this strong-willed child who already had headstrong ideas, slowly became more and more rebellious in spirit. I didn't know what life was supposed to look like as so called "normal". It never felt normal to me.

Around the age of eight, I was molested several times and in later years it was discovered that I was not alone in this horror. This abuse set me up mentally as a wounded child that would later become a teen of rebellion. I developed a victim mentality that would rule my life for many years. Yes, I certainly was a victim, but without a healing hand to navigate me through that darkness I was to remain a victim for many years to come. I was thirty-two years old before I told anyone of my sexual abuse. This victimization, without healing, set me up to be a receiver of more sexual abuse through my early teen years and emotional and physical abuse in my early and mid-twenties. There is a difference between having been a victim of an abuse and living a life with a victim mentality, as I discovered for myself through the years. I will explain later.

I began to partake more and more into risky behaviors which included smoking at age eleven, and sexual promiscuity by age twelve. My mother became very concerned for me though she did not know about my sexual activity at first. I think she may have suspected it. Her sister, my aunt, lived in Arkansas. They spoke about the issues my mom was having with me and it was decided that we would move to Arkansas to try and change the course of my seemingly inevitable self-destruction.

At age twelve we packed up and headed to Arkansas. I was not happy at all. I was a city girl who was going from the suburbs of Denver to the rural country life of an unknown third world country where people spoke funny, as far as I was concerned. Being in a whole unique and unusual way of life than we were accustomed to, Mom tried so hard to make it fun and an adventure for all of us kids. For a short while it was. She did everything within her power to engage me into learning and growing and discovering this whole new world of country living. Mom eventually had to work long hard hours at the Queen Wilhelmina Inn as a cook. We lived 5 miles East of Mena and Mom had to travel 13 miles west of Mena, Arkansas up a winding road to the State Park located on Rich Mountain the second largest mountain in Arkansas.

Mom's days of working twelve hours and then driving there and back made it hard for her to care for the family by herself. Much of the responsibility fell upon my shoulders to help care for my siblings. Though I loved them very much, I was a tween and budding into my soon- to-be teens. The last thing I wanted to do was babysit all the time. I became bored and rebellious. I began to take off and leave, going here and there. And so, my troubles began. For my mother, well let's just say that I gave that woman every gray hair on her head for which I am so very sorry.

As I began to take off and be gone, my mother would look desperately for me. Sometimes she would find me in obvious places like the Bear Cat Pool Hall in Mena and sometimes searching and never finding me. Oh, how fearful she must have been, as I am looking back. Little did she know that I was in situations that I myself was fearful of too. I was too prideful and stubborn to back away and so I pressed onward plunging deeper into the darkness.

My mother was diligent in trying to keep me corralled, but to no avail. I recall one specific day that she had gone to town to get me and bring me home, only for me to take off and go again as soon as I was out of the car. In her frustration, she would call the sheriff and have them pick me up and bring me home. The officer would leave and as soon as he was out of sight I would run down to the end of the lane where my friend with a truck was waiting and I would jump in and go again. Mom would call the sheriff again. This played out until the sheriff got frustrated and basically started to threaten to lock me up. The last time he dropped me off, my friends no longer wanted to come and get me and I still did not want to stay home. I saddled up my horse whose name was PX which was short for Pony Express. I figured in my little mind that if I took the horse to town that they could not put the horse in the car and they would leave me alone. Wrong! My mother was as stubborn as I was. (I wonder where I got it from?)

I rode to town and went to the pool hall where my friends hung out. I tied my horse up outside under a tree like the Wild West hitching post. I went on in to have my fun. As I was shooting pool, the sheriff came in and tapped me on the back once again and I turned around. He now knowing me well said, "Vera, come on. This is getting old and this is the last time I am taking you home." I smiled big and with a smug attitude said to him, "But you can't take me home because I brought my horse. How will I get it home?" He looked a bit surprised and said, "Show me." I walked outside and took him around the side of the pool hall and took him to where I had my horse shaded. He shook his head and radioed to dispatch that they would need to call my mother to come and get me because he could not fit the horse into his car. I thought I had won finally, but my mother's determination would win out that day.

Mom came into town with her old 1960's Thunderbird while the sheriff waited with me and the horse until she got there. Once there, she made me get on the horse and had her friend hold the reigns from inside the car. We drove at a slow trot and walk at times, all the way home. I conceded to my formidable adversary that day. Mom had won. Of course, I was grounded, but that was only as good as her ability to first catch me or to find me.

This was the beginning of the escalation of behaviors that only became riskier and more dangerous. Through hanging at the pool hall, I ended up meeting an older group of people. These people though they appeared nice by day, in fact became dangerous by night. It did not take long to be sucked into a very dark hole. It was one of great evil and honestly it was a miracle that I survived this period of my life. There is absolutely no doubt in my mind that the Lord's protective hands were snuggly around me.

I met a man named Bobby. I thought he was very cute and I wanted a boyfriend. I was very mature physically for my age and I dressed seductively as was common for the mid 1970's. No twelve-year-old child should have been wearing what I was wearing or hanging out where I was hanging out. It only invited trouble. Bobby began to show interest in me and me in him. He began to treat me as though I was his girlfriend although it was never spoken as such.

In my mind, I wanted to have someone to love me and I wanted to love someone in return. I needed someone to understand me, which he seemed to do. I was sucked into that old victim mentality again and was willing to sacrifice myself for the love I was searching for. I would do what Bobby asked without question even if I was uncomfortable doing as he asked. We did have a sexual relationship and he never made me feel loved. I always walked away feeling used and empty and I was. This person was no boy. He was not a teen. He was a man. In those days, he would not have been in trouble for what he was doing. In these days, he would be called a pedophile, a sexual predator and child rapist. Bobby was twenty-three years old and I was twelve years old.

Bobby did drugs and introduced me to doing them on a routine basis. I had been around drugs before and dabbled a little bit before his introduction to me. It had become a daily way of life along with the use of alcohol. I did not enjoy doing either of them, but I wanted to fit in and be a part of the group of adults that I hung with. I felt the pressure to do as they did. So, I did.

All along the way, I was given ways out of the situations I was involved in. Doors opened where I could have walked away, but I chose to stay. Many times, I was given choices that would have prevented me from being involved. I think it was God giving me an out in this shadowy world, but I continued to stay. I would have the thoughts in my head of the enemy telling me that I would have fun and it would get better. I would listen and proceed forward. I made bad choices at every fork in the road I came to, it seemed.

The parties became more and more, as did the drugs and alcohol. The time came that trust had been established within the group. It was determined by the group that I was loyal to them and so I could be trusted to carry out some things to make myself more valuable to the group. They began to teach me how to drive. I thought this was great fun. But their motive was not for fun but for a very monetary purpose. I was being groomed to drive the car for the couriering of alcohol from Oklahoma into Arkansas.

We lived in a dry county and so we would need to boot-leg the alcohol from point A to point B. To have kids drive the car that carried the alcohol was a smart move on the adults' part because very little was done by the law if and when a child underage was caught with the goods. I did get caught once when I first started. I was arrested and then taken to the police station but the sheriff just called my mother to come and get me and then of course I was threatened to be locked up forever if it were to happen again. I did do it again and again but did not get caught again. I do not know if what the sheriff told me was true or not. But I certainly took the chance.

We would drive across the state line into Oklahoma via West of De Queen, Arkansas. We went to the two bars that were there and buy all we could from each bar. Whatever they could spare. They usually had plenty enough to fill our trunk and back seat as this was a regular run. We would fill our vehicle and then we would stay and party at the bar until it closed and then head back to Mena.

The bars that we were in were not legally able to serve liquor. They were licensed to serve beer only. Liquor was served in plastic cups. If the police showed up, the lookout would alert the owners. They would click the lights on and off numerous times inside the bar and everyone knew to discard the liquor. Everyone rushed to make sure they did not have any in their possession to avoid being arrested.

I made this run numerous times and my poor mother never knew where to even begin to look for me anymore. I cannot imagine how much pain and fear I had caused her, even though in later years I would suffer the same such pain of my own, with my son. I do not know how to compare the pain of one mother to that of another. All I know is my mother was aging fast and she was forlorn in appearance and appeared to be hopeless and helpless to do anything. I knew she looked broken, but it was not until I experienced my own pain as a mother of a meth addict in later years, was I able to understand some of her pain.

On one of my last runs to Oklahoma I recall a deal going bad and it scared me so much I ended up calling out to the God I once knew as a child. I was witnessing things that I had not seen in such a degree before. I had witnessed domestic violence before, but I had never witnessed an attempted murder until now. I was sitting in the car waiting as Bobby and his friend were loading the car with the booze as usual, when an intoxicated man came up to the car and started flirting with me. He would not back down when I asked him to go away. Being the shy and withdrawn person I was in those days, I just locked my door and kept saying to myself, "Come on Bobby, come on." He finally came out the door and realized that someone was bothering me while I sat in the car.

Bobby walked up to the car and put the booze in the trunk and walked around to the driver's side of the car where the man stood by me as I was sitting in the driver's seat. Bobby at first just said, "Hey buddy, what's up?" The guy got smart with him and so Bobby told him to get away from me, as I was his girlfriend. The man refused to move.

Bobby then laid his left hand on the man's shoulder and the man took a swing at Bobby going under his arm with his right hand. Bobby backed up and grabbed his chest. He began running backwards. The man pursued him swinging and Bobby kept running. Bobby's friend came out of the bar and saw something was happening. He dropped his booze and ran to aide Bobby in the "fight". Bobby screamed at his friend, "Stay back! He has a knife!" When people heard that, a lot of men surrounded the man with the knife and under the Illumination of the street lamp it became evident that the man indeed had a knife in his hand. He started waving it around and turning in the circle of men he was surrounded by, as if to invite whoever wanted a piece of him to come on in the circle and try.

Someone screamed the police were on their way and this distracted the man briefly. Bobby's friend then kicked the man's hand and the knife went flying in the air to the ground. Someone grabbed the knife and the crowd subdued the man. As I watched this play out from the car, I was petrified and wished so badly that I was not in this situation. But again, I had too much pride and possibly was too fear stricken to remove myself from these types of situations.

Bobby was doubled over holding his chest and the darkness had not yet revealed the evil truth of the situation. The bar tender ran out to Bobby as I was trying to get out and go that direction, as I felt it was now safe. She yelled at me to get into the back seat of my car because the friend of Bobby needed to drive to the nearest hospital, as fast as he could. I did not have that kind of experience. I did as she instructed me to do. She helped Bobby into the back seat with me. He looked pale and was not doing very well. The woman then told me, "You put lots of pressure on this rag and don't you let up a bit! Keep him talking and don't let him stop!"

When Bobby's friend opened the car and the light came on, it became evident to me that Bobby was dying. He leaned into me, looked up at me and said, "I'm dying. I am going to die." I put intense pressure on the bar rags that were blood soaked on the left side of his chest. I screamed, "No! No, you are not going to die! Not tonight!" I pushed him back upright and leaned into him to secure his rags to his chest. I was wearing a white skirt and I was covered in blood that did not seem to quit coming from him no matter how hard I was trying. The woman slammed the door shut and screamed to the driver, "Go! Go! Go Now!" The driver put it into gear and put the gas petal to the floor. We topped well over 100 miles per hour and I was scared we would all die.

I remember praying to God, "Please Lord, don't let him die, don't let us die. Help us Lord God, please help us!" I was frantic and just wanted my mother, but I knew that if I were ever going to act like an adult, now was the time to do it. This mans' life was now in my hands, literally. I recall the stickiness of his blood as it began to dry and clot running down my arms and hands, the look of hopelessness in his eyes, as he knew he was about to die and the belief in my heart that he was right. It was all too surreal.

The hand of God was upon us all as we made our way to the Mena Hospital. We were never stopped by the police driving the way we were. When we got to the hospital, Bobby's friend had the good sense to tell me, "You cannot be seen in the middle of all of this. You have to go and hide in those bushes." I cried and said to him, "But I need to stay with him! What if he dies?" The friend said, "Vera, if he dies this is a murder case. You cannot be involved. Now go and do as I say! Hide! I will come and keep you updated as to what is going on. Now go!" His friend did as he said he would. As I sit behind the bushes in the darkness all I could do was pray. I did not know what to pray other than "Help me Lord. Help Bobby." I was alone, scared and had no one to guide me from this very dark and evil place I had plummeted into. My life seemed to be playing out in slow motion.

This night was long and yet it was quickly turning into day light. I needed to figure out what to do, not to be seen. Bobby's friend came to me and said he called a female friend of his that was coming to get me. She would take me to her house so that I could shower and change clothes. He reported to me that Bobby was stabilized and on life support, as the knife wound was deep enough that it punctured his lung. The doctor was confident that he would live and he did.

I remember thanking God for saving his life. The strange thing is that not until now did I even think about the fact that most victims would have wanted their perpetrator to die. I did not even realize at that time in my life that I was with a child rapist and he was not my boyfriend. How deceived we can be when we are surrounded by darkness.

Bobby went on to recover and we continued our Oklahoma runs once he got back on his feet, at least for a little while longer. My time in Mena was a brief time in that I left there when I was almost 14 years old. Many more stories could be told of this time that led to where the Lord finally stepped in and said, "Enough!"

For the sake of the length of this book, I think you have gotten the picture of where I was headed and how turbulent the times were. There was no doubt that I was smack dab in the middle of Satan's dominion and surrounded by his minions. I had absolutely no one to pull me out because I would not listen to the only person who truly loved me and that was my mother. She finally had to give up and sacrifice me to spare the other four kids from the hell I was bringing upon our family. She gave me up to God. I do believe, that there was not a day, or periods in the day that my mother was not praying for me.

Long story short, I had quit school at age 13 and lived in a boarding house. The owner was a sweet man that began to be an angel for my mother as he would keep her informed as to what I was doing and how I was doing. Mom knew she could not make me go home because I would just run away again. We ended up going to court due to truancy issues from school. Judge Bus Stephenson, a godly man I do believe, was placed in my path to assist God in redirecting my path. He was firm with me in court and knowing my issues all too well, he still allowed me a choice. He told me that I could continue to live on my own and stay at the boarding house with Dallas who owned it, only if I would continue to go to school. Of course, I completely agreed to the conditions. The judge made it clear that if I did not go to school then he was taking over and not even my mother could help me.

I was in the seventh grade and so back to school I went. I did well for a while. I had managed to break away from Bobby. He did not want the light of a court room shining anywhere near him. I got involved with some college kids that were partying all the time. Bad choice. This made it hard to go to school the next day. Dallas tried to wake me for school each day, knocking on my door but I refused to get up and go. It did not take long before I was back in court and then placed in the custody of the State of Arkansas and placed into foster care. A mixed blessing to my mother. A total blessing for me, although at the time I did not believe it to be. And a complete miracle of God who took the reins and pulled me out of that darkness and placed me into the home of Kathy and Lacey, my new foster parents.

I love them to this day because they took my hands and led me back to the Lord. The Lord of Mr. Mullins and of Mr. Owl, to the roots of my teachings. It did not take me long, listening to the pastor week after week of how the Lord had truly been with me through the darkest period of my life up to that point. I knew I needed Him to be my Lord and Savior. For the first time in my stubborn life I made an excellent choice.

I had accepted Jesus Christ as my Lord and Savior, submitting to his Lordship over me. Without him I would have either died or continued in the darkness and who knows how it would have ended? I knew in my heart that it was God that had carried me out of the darkness and gave me the brilliant light of Jesus! Did I live happily ever after, having become a child of God? Why no! I still had some growing to do. I still had the immature character traits I had a few moments before I had asked Him into my heart. But what I did have after I asked Him to be my Lord, was God's grace, mercy and love like I had never known before. It was now up to me to seek God with all my heart and learn who God was and learn who I was in God's eyes.

I still had choices to make along the way. I still made some bad choices which took me into depression and darkness again and again, but this time I was taking someone with me everywhere I went. His name was Jesus!

Becoming a Christian does make us immediately perfect, especially in the eyes of humans. But I was made perfect in the righteousness of Jesus Christ and that was all I needed in God's eyes!

My journey to mature in Christ has been a long and turbulent one. However, God has never given up on me. Have I disappointed him? Absolutely. Have I appeared as though I was a hypocrite to others at times? Absolutely. Have I ever, fallen hard in my walk? Yes, I certainly have. But just like a baby learning to walk, I being a new Christian had to learn how to walk in my new Christian faith. I had to learn to be obedient to the God I had made Lord over my life.

I have at times regressed and fell flat on my bottom. But like a good daddy would, God reached down and grabbed my hand, dusted off my bottom and told me to try again. He gave me the grace to try again! Why? Because, "There is no condemnation for those who love Christ Jesus." The bible is clear we are "sealed" and we are his! What human father would ever spank their 2-year-old child for falling as they were learning to walk? None that I know of, so why would God spank us as we are learning to walk in our new spiritual life with him? I don't believe that he would.

Many stories could be told about the rest of my teen years of situations that occurred in my life and where I had to make choic-es and didn't always do so well. However, it will have to be told another day. Know this, God put me in a home with people who were not perfect people, but they loved God and did their best to love me too despite myself. To this day nearly thirty-five years later, I still have them included into my life because they helped to change my life. They listened to the Lord. When I was not an easy child to love, they chose to love me anyway. "Greater love hath no man than he lay down his life for a friend." They chose to die to themselves to save me. I love them so very much for their sacrifices which were many.

Remember, just because I accepted Jesus didn't mean I didn't remain strong-willed and stubborn. God had to retrain me over time. Sometimes I had to be disciplined in love and sometimes I had to fall hard to learn (Hebrews 5:8). I still have struggles and stubbornness and a very strong will. I have learned to control it more than I did way back then, but I still have my moments of humanness. I know that the Lord walks with me now, everywhere that I go. And sometimes, God must pick me up when I fall, because I still do on occasion.

It is not necessary for me to summarize in this chapter what I learned or who walked me out of the darkness, as it is clear. The evidence shows that God walked with me throughout these times of my life. I believe, God placed angels about me where ever I went. I will say however, that though I was saved by the Lord Jesus Christ I still had battles that lay ahead of me. All that I had suffered up to this point was grooming me for what lie ahead. Had I not grown and learned from where I had come from, I would not be ready to accept the challenges of the future. I did not know this back then. I finally did realize just how much all I had gone through would serve me later in life. I still say, not a thing would I change because it made me who I am today.

My life's journeys have refined my character growth and taught me to love others the way I want to be loved. I do not love others the way they want loved, but the way I want loved and how God loved me. If I loved others the way they wanted loved, they would not receive what they needed. I learned that the love I had searched for and ultimately gained was harmful and wasn't love at all. It was not what I needed, but it was what I thought I wanted and ultimately needed. I was wrong, as I will prove in my next testimony of my life in the twenties.

I am going to give two more scenarios in my life. This is not to drag on and bore you. I do this that I might be able to reach out and expand to a broader audience to identify with in certain situations, which may afford them the hope that they too can overcome the darkness. I only share the skeletons of my closet so that God can be glorified and that others may see that there is hope in this dark world. Transparency is never easy. We risk having it used against us when we are transparent. It is a risk that I am willing to make, to honor God and to help others overcome their life circumstances.

Each time that my light would grow dim, as I entered the darkness of the next battle, I would become stronger and more alert to the fact that I was to learn something. I ultimately, would emerge with a light that would shine just a little bit brighter than it did before the battle. It equipped me for the next battle that lay ahead. It equipped me to help others, which gave my life meaning and purpose. We all need to have a purpose to live life to the fullest and to feel valued.

CHAPTER 4

DOMESTIC ABUSE

AFTER ONE FAILED marriage to my high school sweetheart, I felt totally like a failure myself. He was a wonderful person and yet we simply did not have the skills to overcome the adult situations in our lives. We were married five days after my eighteenth birthday. We were too young to handle what life was throwing at us and circumstances won and love lost. I do treasure my teen years dating him as he showed me how a man should treat a woman and what love was all about. Up to that point it was very fuzzy to me in my life. He brought a sense of normality to my life, but I brought chaos to his sadly.

Not long after that marriage dissolved I met another man, Cliff, he was ten years my senior. He was exciting and fun. He was just finishing up his years as a bare-back rider in the rodeo. The life style was tremendously exhilarating and addictive to be around. I never wanted it to end. It did not take long however before it did end due to numerous reasons. The party began to fade but the alcohol and drugs that were the center of it all did not. I had fallen in love with this man and overlooked so many things to justify my feelings for him. I could see in him what others could not. What I learned the hard way was that seeing potential in someone does not create the result unless they can see the potential in themselves. He could not.

Cliff could not open and tell me how he felt unless he was very drunk. If it was on beer, then I could at least hear the pain that drove his self-destruction. But if it was whiskey that he was drinking, then it was a for sure thing that abuse and violence would prevail. His pain would rage in violent behaviors rather than released words. The roller coaster ride had begun and I for some reason could not allow myself to get off. Sometimes as I reflect on these times, I consider that maybe I was trying to punish myself for all that I had done to others. I felt that I deserved what I was getting. I went from being an independent, do as I wish person, to a very submissive, quiet and withdrawn person. I apologized for every breath I took, if it meant keeping the peace with him.

My parents tried to get me to leave so many times because they could see the changes in me. They knew that I was suffering some abuse but they did not know the extent to which it was. In the beginning, I did not know why it would happen or when it would happen, but over time I began to figure out the pattern. Then when I anticipated that it was building tension and would blow I would purposely try to push a button to make it blow, to get it over with. I just wanted peace. I knew that once he blew up and did his thing that there would be a period where things were good and he was remorseful. I could again see the potential and the man that I had fallen in love with which gave me hope that we would work it all out and life would be good. I was uneducated in this area of domestic violence. Little did I know; I was in what is called the Cycle of Abuse. The escalation period would lead to the explosion period, which would then lead to the honeymoon period which I craved so much. We seemed to cycle quickly as round and round we went.

One day I found out that I was pregnant and I was so excited! All I could think of was that I would finally have some little person that would love me unconditionally and I would love them back the same. I had this fantasy that all would be well now and that even this might fix the problems in our relationship because now we would have a family. I could not wait to get off work to run and tell Cliff the good news. I was so very happy. I went to the Four Seasons Bar where I knew he would be, to tell him. Thinking he would be happy too, I blurted it out with great excitement and anticipation of how he would react. Never in a million years did I think he would blow up the way he did when he found out. It was terrible and devastating to me. He demanded that I end the pregnancy immediately. I refused and decided that I would leave him and I did. He constantly tried to contact me to try and talk me into getting an abortion which was against all that I believed in and I refused to allow him to wear me down. So, I went to a friend's home and I hid there for about five months and never spoke to Cliff at all during that time.

One day a friend of mine talked me into going out to dance, to the very place Cliff hung out. I knew better but I felt strong enough now that I was past the stage of legal abortion that I could handle things should I run into him. As I was paying to enter the dance area someone came up and grabbed me from behind and swung me around and said, "Oh my God! Where have you been?" It was Cliff. He went on to say that he was wrong and that he was sorry. He had been too scared to face being a father again. He was older than me. He already had kids from a previous marriage and he had never considered starting all over again. He continued with many more convincing words and my heart melted as I began to believe him. I wanted a family and I wanted my baby to have his daddy there. I gave in and we reconciled our relationship.

The struggle became difficult because Cliff could not and would not hold a job. I could not get a job because I was near due date and no one would hire me. We lived off pinto beans and chocolate pudding that he would sneak from his mom's house. I was too prideful to ask for help from my family because I knew how they felt about him not working. One day my mom and my uncle Mike came to town. They were trucking partners and were coming through Denver. When they saw the situation that we were living in, my uncle said for us to pack up and get into the Semi with them. They were taking us to Kansas so I could be with my mom to have the baby. We did not argue. We packed immediately and away we went. Then on August 3, 1983 I gave birth to a 10 pound 3-ounce baby boy who was 22 inches long. He was perfect!

Even the perfection of this beautiful baby boy could not heal the brokenness within my husband. He loved our son very much. When the two of them were alone and I would watch from another room or from a window, I could see the love that he had for him. It broke my heart that whatever the issue or pain that was inside of Cliff had caused so much damage, even the promise of new life could not heal it. It did not take long before the drinking and drugs became worse and worse. This led to an increase of domestic abuse. He was not physical with his abuse in the beginning. It was more the emotional and mental abuse. He would intimidate a lot then. Nothing that I did was ever good enough for him it seemed. He constantly accused me of cheating when I never left the house. I could never understand why I could not help him fight his demons inside. I did not even know for many years where the pain was coming from.

The cycle continued for twelve long, hard years. It only escalated and became more violent. I became more submissive and meek. I was fearful of every move I made. Fearful that I would make the wrong decision or choice in any given situation. I was terrified to make a decision for fear it would blow things up.

Five years after our first son was born I became pregnant again. September 17, 1988 my precious son weighing in at 9 pounds 5 ounces and 21 inches long came into my life. It was another fight to keep my baby, as it was the first one. In fact, he left me for six months and then returned when he decided he had made a mistake and was feeling remorseful. I cannot tell you how many times that he left me and I allowed him to come back. It was like a yo-yo effect. One year he left me 14 times. I had been conditioned to believe that I was not valuable and I deserved everything I was getting. I believed that no one would ever love me or want me if I was not with Cliff. If I wanted a complete family it had to be with him. I had to be grateful if he returned home. I was wrong, but this was what I had grown to believe.

Prior to my second son being born the violence had escalated. He was beating me physically and bringing blood. I was very scared and I would call the police every time. At that time, there were no domestic violence laws in Kansas. That was the last night I called the police for help for a very long time. I heard the officer in the living room with my husband telling him how he understood what Cliff was going through. The officer stated, "Yeah, my wife is a bitch when she is pregnant too." He then came into the bedroom where I sat bloody and beaten, holding my oldest son tight, who was terrified of what he was witnessing. The officer stated to me, "If I have to keep coming out here I will take your kids. Do you understand me?" I understood all too well. I could not call for help anymore and I would have to take whatever my husband doled out or leave. I refused to leave. I did not want to be a failure again at marriage. I wanted to find a way to make this marriage work and have the happy family I dreamed of.

I began to turn back to the Lord from whom I had hidden myself from in shame. I needed someone and was too prideful to reach out to family and I had been isolated from friends. I began to go to a little church in Kipp, Kansas. My boys and I were accepted with open arms and with so much love. It was a very tiny church with very few people, but the people there were wonderful and most were elderly with great wisdom and strength. They began to help me heal and to learn that the Lord loved me no matter what I had done. He had enough grace and mercy to cover it all. I rededicated my life back to Christ and began to teach my children about Jesus. This brought some peace to our lives that we so desperately needed. When the storms would come, then Jesus would calm the waters. Things didn't seem as bad when we focused on Him even though the abuse did not stop.

The more we got closer to God the more distant Cliff became toward us. I finally realized that he knew that there was not enough room in the house for the demons inside of him and our Lord Jesus Christ who was now living inside of us and our home. Once again Cliff moved out. This time it was a longer period which was good for my healing.

I worked as a cosmetologist in Salina, Kansas. I did not make very much but did the best that I could to support my boys. I needed extra help here and there, so I was a recipient of some state support. I was standing at the WIC office waiting to get my WIC checks in a long line with other women. It was humiliating for me and I just wanted to get in and get out like always because I did not want someone that I knew to see me getting handouts. Did I mention that I was prideful? One of my worst character traits for sure. As I stood there in line there was a woman standing by a table alongside the wall and she gently smiled at me and asked me to come and talk to her. I respectfully declined because I did not want to lose my place in line. She assured me that I would not if I would just give her a couple minutes of my time.

Little did I know but this was where the Lord was sending in some more help to navigate me out of the dark. First, it was the little church with the church women who simply loved me. Now, it was this woman standing at a table, by a chance happening. Or was it by chance?

She asked me if I was happy in life or if I felt that I had room to make more happiness in my life. Of course, who wouldn't want more happiness? I knew we sure could use some. So, I gave her the response that she knew I would and told her we could use some more of course. She asked me if I had ever considered going to college. I told her I had gone to technical school and was a beautician but that I was barely making it because beauticians were a dime a dozen. It was a hard way to make money, but I tried. She asked me again and then emphasized the difference between a technical school and college. I told her that I was not smart enough to go to college because I barely made it out of high school. She offered me a deal. She said that she would be willing to pay for one college class for me, to prove that I was smart enough. If I would take the class and do well, then I must promise to sign up and go to college. The state had a program at that time for single mothers and single fathers to go to school. The state would pay for it if I maintained a certain grade point average (GPA).

I was very hesitant. She kept telling me that I had nothing to lose and everything to gain. If I failed, then I didn't lose anything but some of my time. If I did well, I had a whole new future ahead of me, for me and my sons. Well, all a person had to say is that I would be doing this for my children and that was it. Challenge accepted. I would go and prove her wrong, I thought in my head. She set up a time to meet at my home to sign up for everything and we met. It was a done deal.

My husband and I kept in touch as he lived in Salina, only a few miles away. He laughed at me when he heard what I was doing and told me I was way too stupid to do this and in my heart, I believed he was right. I just knew in my heart that I needed to try for my sons. I wanted a better life for them and this was my one time shot at it.

In spite of the ridicule and my own self-doubt, I signed up for the class and went to college one night a week. It was wonderful getting out of the house and having some "adult" time. I was surprised as to how much fun learning was now in my life since I hated school so much growing up. I enjoyed the class and the people I had grown to like. When time came for the grades to be handed out, I was so shocked to find that I had received an A for my grade. This meant that I had to be a person of my word and it looked like college was in my future.

It was to be a very long and difficult two years which included summers, as I entered college to become a nurse. I shed many tears as I found the classes that I would take, were much harder than the class the lady had me take. I felt that I had been duped. I wanted to quit many times as this was the hardest thing that I had ever done for myself or my children. But teachers would encourage me to push on and gave me extra help when I needed it.

I was terrible at math and failed it in the regular college classes. Finally, someone told me about a junior college that offered the classes in our county. They held them at our high schools in the area and that I should consider them. I did just that. I found that there was one at the school where my oldest son went and so I signed up. One of the high school teachers taught the class and was willing to bring it down to my level of understanding and help me move up to the level of growth I needed to be at. I will forever be grateful to Mr. Bob Sauber, who without his kind, gentle, patient and caring way of teaching I would have never graduated from college. He was a navigator in my life as well. He will never know the impact he made on my life. My deepest respect and admiration is for him. It takes a very special person to be a teacher. To him I am forever grateful.

I went on to graduate and became a nurse. It was very hard on my kids while I went to school. I worked full time, went to school full time and for a year raised my sister's kids too, to help her out. I had five kids ages 6, 5, 4, and two 2-year-old children by my last year of college. But by the grace of God, we made it. I had learned to make some decisions and not fear the outcome as much. I began to have some self-confidence again and I was coming out of the shell of that meek, scared little girl I had regressed to before college. I was becoming an overcomer. I was starting to shed my victim mentality.

My husband still did not live at home. He remained like background noise and only became more critical of me. He was feeling that I was pulling away from him due to my growth and his insecurity. What he didn't understand was that he had already pulled away from us. I continued to just keep growing as he remained stagnant. I just knew that I could not stay in that stagnant state of mind. I had to grow whether he chose to or not. With growth comes pain sometimes. Watching the person that you love stay stagnant was painful to watch because not only did I love him, but I knew his full potential. It was painful to watch him waste it away on alcohol and drugs. We did end up back together for a time after I graduated. It did not last long. I tried to encourage him to go to college too, but he refused. I tried to get him to go to church with us, but again he refused. I even tried to check out the Mormon church that he said he had grown up in to see if that would be something that would draw us back together, but that did not work either. His pain ran deep and there was no reaching him. I simply did not have enough knowledge to help him. I knew he loved me the best he knew how. All I could do was pray for him.

The fights were getting closer and closer together. Sometimes by phone and sometimes when he came over to visit the kids.

Eventually, after I had graduated, I allowed Cliff to move back home, but the cycle of abuse became more frequent. The abuse more abusive and the violence more violent. One day after he had some mild physical abuse and a lot of emotional and mental abuse towards me while I had been washing dishes, my mind began reeling in anger, like I had not experienced before.

I began fantasizing of what it would be like to dominate him and make him feel what I was having to endure. As I continued to wash the silverware with robust strokes, I could feel the rage only intensify in my mind. Then with the large clean knife in my hand I walked into my bedroom where my husband stood at the closet, as if nothing had just happened. I just stood there staring at him. He turned around and said, "What do you want?" I did not respond. He then got sarcastic and said, "What's wrong with you? Are you crazy?" I then responded, "Why yes I am. Right this very minute I could stab you with this knife in the gut and feel absolutely nothing." The look on his face was of fear and he knew that he had finally pushed me to the edge and I knew it too. I calmly turned around and went back to washing dishes and he never said another word to me again that night. I began to pray because I did not like the person that I just witnessed in me. I did not like the darkness that I knew could take me down the wrong road if I was to follow through with the thoughts that were going through my tormented mind. I knew that it was time to get out.

It was to be our last fight as a married couple as Easter arrived. I was so very sick with strep throat and I could not even get out of bed. I was on an antibiotic but just could not play the Easter bunny that year. I told my sons that the Easter bunny had called and had gotten stuck in the North with the snow and that he should be here in a day or two and to please forgive him. The boys were very understanding and though they were disappointed, they knew the Easter bunny would keep his word and come.

Cliff had been gone all day drinking with friends and came home late that evening very drunk on whiskey. He tried in the best way he could to carry on a conversation with the boys wanting to know what the Easter bunny had brought them. He became enraged when he found out that we had not celebrated Easter due to me being sick and the yelling began. He said, "What kind of mother would do this to their children?" It went downhill from there.

I told him I was too sick to fight, but he would not stop. I tried to get up off the couch to go to my room but he would not allow that. He ended up backing me up into the corner of the living room and I knew what was about to happen. I was so very sick and just didn't have it in me to receive what he was about to give. I closed my eyes, doubled up my fist and I punched straight forward hitting him in the nose. It was by pure luck that I even made contact. He staggered back and then grabbed his nose with such a shocked look on his face, as this was the very first time in twelve years that I physically responded to his abuse. I knew in my heart that I was about to really get it bad, now that I had done that. So, I thought to myself I better hit him again and this time I purposely hit him in the nose again to stop him from coming at me. He was drunk enough that the shock of me doing this caused him to give me time to escape the corner. I called the police for the first time in years because I knew it would escalate.

The police arrived and to my shock and dismay, I was arrested. Yes, that very year evidently a new domestic violence law had gone into effect and the first person to make physical contact was the one that was arrested. I could not believe what I was hearing. Twelve years of abuse and numerous calls for help and no one would arrest him. But the one time I finally stand up for myself, I am arrested for domestic battery. I was in total disbelief. The officers that came were very kind and allowed me to call my mother to come and get the boys since Cliff was drunk. They waited with me there at the house for her to arrive. They also agreed not to handcuff me until my mom left with the boys so that they would not be traumatized by what they were seeing. My mother bailed me out of jail and I had a set court date to go to that week. I could not believe that this was happening.

I went to court and the judge was not a nice person. I did not understand the proceeding process and he kept asking me if I wanted to plead innocent or guilty. I would try to explain the situation and he would cut me off and said I was either innocent or guilty and that was all he wanted to hear. I would try again to explain and again he would repeat what he said before. I did not realize that I would get an appointed lawyer and come back for court if I would just say not guilty. I was ignorant of the process. I knew I had hit him, but there were reasons that I felt threatened, due to the history and I felt it was self-defense. This judge would not explain that I could explain all of this if I would just plead not guilty. Because I knew I had hit him and by not understanding the process, in pure frustration I said, "I guess I am guilty then! I did hit him but to protect myself." The judge entered the plea of guilty and sentenced me to six months in the county jail suspended with a year probation. I was also to enter anger management classes!

This was a bad dream! Twelve years of abuse by an angry man and I have to take anger management classes?! I was beside myself with that sentence and my old self crept back into the picture and before I could gain self-control I blurted out to the judge, "If I had known I would be sentenced like this I would have punched him harder and made it count!" The judge found no humor in that statement and nor did I mean any humor. I was very upset. He let me know that I was close to receiving a contempt charge and I would be doing myself a favor to hold my tongue. Which I might add is sometimes difficult for me to do. Hold my tongue that is, but I managed to accomplish it that day. I did not want to make matters worse.

As I drove home I realized the total impact of what had just happened. I knew that if I stayed with my husband that we would have another argument or fight sooner or later. I also knew that being on probation, if something happened that we did fight, then I would have my probation revoked and I would be sitting in the county jail for six months. I would lose my nursing career, my children, my home, my job and my life as I knew it. I would not lose my children. It came time to make a hard decision. He was going. Long story short, I went home and helped him to move his belongings out immediately. He could not understand why. This was my second time to initiate his leaving in this twelve year period. I was done. We ended up divorced.

The damage had been done. Not only to me but to my children who endured it for as long as they did. It would come back to be many more dark times ahead with my children as they learned to overcome the years of abuse they had witnessed and the verbal abuse they endured themselves. Not to mention my own depression and isolation that made them feel isolated and alone themselves. I did not know how to cope and I did not know how to help my children cope. But guess what? I had an anger management class that I was about to begin and ironically, I was angry about having to attend.

It did not take too many weeks into the class to realize that it was a God intervention that I desperately needed. Not only did it teach me how to feel emotions and identify them correctly it taught me how to respond rather than to react. But the greatest thing it helped me to understand was why I did what I did, my behaviors. I could not tell you how many times in my life that I had reacted a certain way and then would get angry at myself because I behaved that way and I wanted to know why I did that! This class was the right class at the right time. It gave me the answers I had searched for most of my life. It was a biblical based psycho-educational class that taught me skills to rise above circumstances. It gave me insight into my own behaviors and the behaviors of others, which allowed me to learn to forgive others and myself.

I learned a lot in the Life Skills Class and thanks to Dr. Paul Hegstrom, I went on to help my children heal and many of my extended family took the class as well. I decided that this was something that I wanted to share with others. I knew that if I had suffered this kind of emotional pain that others must have gone through similar issues too. I decided to become a facilitator for the Life Skills Program. It was therapeutic and healing for me as I helped other women who suffered similar issues to become healed. I was no longer the navigated, but rather the one navigating. It was a huge change in my life. It gave me a purpose and feeling of some importance. I finally felt that I had some value. I had something to give.

I opened a Life Skills Center in Salina, Kansas and I taught women at first. I then decided that I wanted to learn more about the men and how to help them. If I could learn to have empathy for them based on why they did what they did, meaning the root of their pain that caused or influenced their behaviors, then I could not only help them, but maybe heal some more of me. It was a way for me to understand my ex-husband and extend to him forgiveness and lift the burdens of shame from my chest. I began teaching the men's batterer's class. It was eye opening and brought me tremendous healing. I learned to love the men that had caused so much pain for so many women and it brought so much joy to help them arrive at their own self-understanding and healing. Though I could never teach my ex-husband these skills and lead him to healing, I could learn forgiveness for him, which I did.

In 2013 I was notified that the boys' dad was dying in California. His years of drinking had finally caught up with him. He was dying of cirrhosis of the liver. I recall crying for many reasons. I cried mostly for my boys who would be losing their dad with unresolved grief and loss from their past. I was crying for what could have been, had alcohol not stolen his life from him. I cried for the emotionally painful life he had suffered silently alone. I cried for his mother and sister who loved him so much and I loved them.

I came to the Lord and prayed, "What should I do?" I knew that his life had been nothing but torment and he was about to die. I knew that he was in a dark place and someone needed to help him navigate into the right direction. I wrote a letter to him telling him how I felt about him. I believed that he was a good man inside, but that his pain was more than he could handle. I told him that I did not hate him. I had loved him, still cared about him and that I forgave him for everything. I wanted him to know that the man I had loved was not the same man that behaved so badly. The two were separate and that God felt the same way. God can separate our sin from who we are, if we would accept the gift of his son, Jesus who paid our debt with his blood.

My youngest son was the only one of us that we could afford to send to California to be with Cliff. My son read the letter to his dad and then had him call me as I had requested. Cliff was initially resistant to this phone call because he knew I had remarried in June of that year. But my son knew where we were heading with all this and he dialed the number and made him call. Cliff was very weak and could not really speak. I told him that he didn't need to speak but that I needed to say some things. My son already told me that Cliff had made everyone leave the room after he had heard my letter. They could hear him crying alone in his room. I knew that this was the moment of truth. His heart was softened and he was not drinking and he had one last choice to make in this life.

I began to reiterate what I had already spoken to him by letter. I went further by telling him that his whole life he lived in torment. I cared enough about him to tell him, that if he would accept Jesus as his savior, that his torment was about to end. He would meet God face to face with everything forgiven. I told him again that I loved him and forgave him and his boys did too. We just want him in Heaven so that someday we can all spend some time being happy around one another. He began to cry. I asked him to accept Jesus as his Lord. Then softly he said, "Jesus, Jesus, Jesus." I told Cliff that was all he had to say because God knows his heart. He was so weak and he spoke the most important words that he had ever spoken in his life! I knew in my heart that the father of my children had just accepted Jesus as his savior. His torment was about to end and happiness for the first time for him, was just over the horizon.

My son who struggles with forgiveness at times, could witness the most amazing moment of forgiveness where his mother forgave his dad. His dad forgave himself too, I pray. Jesus forgave us all and He entered his dad's body to give him eternal peace for the first time. That was a Wednesday, as I recall. My son had to leave the next day to go back to Kansas. It was hard for our son to leave his dad's side because he knew it would be his last time to see him though he tried to encourage his dad to get well so that he could see him when he came to Kansas for a visit. They both knew it would not happen but it made it easier to let go, I believe, for both. On Saturday morning, August 3, 2013 which was my oldest son's

30th birthday, I received a phone call from my ex-brother in-law who informed me that Cliff had passed away.

I cried a lot that morning, but not for myself. I cried this time for the loss that my boys were about to feel. Then I cried happy tears for I knew that Cliff was now safe in the arms of Jesus. The root of his pain was finally gone and he now knew what real joy was. He finally knew what it was to have happiness in his life.

It was a 30-year growing spree for me and for my family. We had suffered much emotional pain through it all, but we learned so much. It forged us in such a way that we all matured in one way or another. We learned what real love was and who the Author of that love was and is. God redeemed from the ashes what was meant for evil and turned it into something that ended up healing many people. You see Cliff's life had meaning. To look at it from what I have written you might think it was a wasted life. Not at all!

Cliff left a legacy. Many hundreds of people were healed because of his pain. Many hundreds of men ended up salvaging their families that they may have otherwise lost had they not come to the Life Skills Classes. Those classes only happened through me because of what we as a family suffered and healed from. The Lord placed many people in my path during that time to navigate me through the dark. God then placed me in position to navigate others through similar pain to help them find hope and healing.

I give all credit and glory to God for all that He did in this time of our lives. I thank Cliff that in the end he made the right choice. Through his life, many have been healed from their pain through the batterer's intervention classes that I taught for many years. Our pain became my purpose to help navigate others into healing similar relationships. I also thank my current husband Mike for having enough understanding to allow our family the closure that we needed to move on in our lives. Cliff loved all his children very much. He simply did not know how to show it. He has 4 wonderful kids, Dylan, Hope, Duley and Dalton (the last two are mine). Cliff missed out on so much wonderful time with them, but sadly the kids missed out as well. They have all grown to be good parents to the best of their ability and I am proud of every one of them.

I have one more testimony to share because I feel it is an important one. However, I want to take a bunny trail to give some understanding of why it is important to understand where behaviors come from. I believe that this little diversion will give you better insight into understanding many of the behaviors we, as a family struggled with and why you may struggle in your own behaviors. This will be a building block to the skills that I will be sharing toward the end of this book. Insight and understanding allow us to make better choices, I do believe.

CHAPTER 5

ARRESTED EMOTIONAL AND SPIRTUAL DEVELOPMENT

I RECALL WHEN I was in foster care in my teens, that I was made to go to counseling with a therapist. It seemed that every discussion that we had, he would ask me, "How do you feel about that?" It would anger me every time. I did not know what I felt and I did not know what I should feel and I certainly did not know how to learn to feel. I would be frustrated that he would ask me that, when I just did not know. I finally told him, "You make the big bucks, you tell me!" All that got me was a diagnosis of Oppositional Defiance Disorder, I suspect.

When that judge court ordered me to the Life Skills Program, I was very mad about it. However, the Lord knew what he was doing. He knew I needed to learn how to feel to move forward. I needed to learn to understand my behaviors and why they manifest the way they do. Learning this would give me insight so that I could not only help myself, but someday help others. He also knew that if I had clarity of understanding in these areas that I would learn how to forgive more easily. I would also learn to understand why God would sacrifice his only son for what I would have called a bunch of losers before I took Life Skills.

I am going to share some of what I learned so many years ago in Life Skills concerning Arrested Emotional Development. Then I will share my theory of what I believe stunts our growth with God because of what I call, Arrested Spiritual Development. I named it for being directly related to the Arrested Emotional Development. It will not be written or discussed in depth here. But I will give you enough information so you will have some understanding of what it is and how it can affect our relationship with God.

ARRESTED EMOTIONAL DEVELOPMENT

The best definition that I can give to this is that when a person has been traumatized at a certain age of development their emotions become stunted in growth at that age. Their chronological age will continue to grow another year older each year, but their emotional growth will not. It will become stagnant at the age of their trauma.

This means if someone is traumatized at age two to three years old, their emotional age will be stunted at that age until such time that healing of that trauma begins. The person may grow up to be twenty-five years old chronologically and seemingly be an adult, but only until such time that stress overload comes into the scene. Once stress is induced, the person who should be acting like an adult of twenty-five will, suddenly, regress to his/her emotional age of two to three years old. When this happens then the behaviors of a child of that age will take over and cause havoc in any relationship. Have you ever said to someone that they were acting like a two-year-old? It is a metaphor we use to describe what we see in one's behaviors when they are not acting their chronological age.

What kind of behaviors might we see in an unhappy two-year-old? Biting, kicking, screaming, crying, hitting, throwing things, breaking things and maybe throwing self on the floor in a temper tantrum hoping to get their own way. Let's now place this behavior in a young adult of either gender who is upset and arrested emotionally at this age. They are under stress and they begin to act out as described. Looks like a possible scenario for domestic abuse and or violence wouldn't you say? It absolutely is. And the only way that the person who is victim to this type of abuse can survive is to set strict limits and personal boundaries and maintain them without giving in. Because just like a two-year-old, if you give in to the bad behaviors then they will continue and may even get worse. These behaviors will not go away completely until the person who is wounded or traumatized gets some direction of how to heal the past hurts.

Erik Erickson who is well known in the world of psychology is known for his theory of the eight stages of psychosocial development. This can be googled to retrieve his work on this topic in its entirety. I won't go through each stage here but it would be worth your time to look it up. You can learn each of the developmental stages and the corresponding age appropriate behaviors. It will give you more insight into your own behaviors in comparison to the stages of psychosocial development and of those around you whom you love. What we understand we can tolerate easier.

I will however share the first stage of Erik Erickson's developmental psychosocial stage of Trust vs Mistrust. If we can complete this stage of development without being wounded or traumatized then we can move forward to the next stage as we age, having a good sense of trust of others. However, if we become wounded due to some traumatic event in our life or our simple needs were not met and we felt rejection then we may develop a sense of mistrust. This means that we will continue to grow and develop moving forward with having a tough time trusting people.

So, let's go back to that twenty-five-year-old who is throwing fits and had domestic violence issues. Now we add the fact that he did not develop a sense of trust in his stage of psychosocial development of Trust vs Mistrust. Not only does he have emotional and behavioral issues, but add to the fire a powerful sense of mistrust. This is a set up for more problems in the relationship. Accusations of infidelity may be thrown at you. It may enhance the fears they have of being abandoned. This may set the stage for stalking the other person in the relationship, due to their fear of abandonment. Can you see how this all is coming together? Can you see why it's important to heal our wounds and do it quickly? Life will not improve until we do. This was a condensed version to help you have some foundational understanding.

For more information on Arrested Emotional Development, I suggest reading Dr. Paul Hegstrom's books, "Broken Children, Grown Up Pain" and "Angry Men and the Women Who Love Them". Dr. Hegstom at the time of proofing this book, has sadly passed away. I attribute to him as being the beacon of light in my dark world, who ultimately brought me to the emerging point of being the light for others through Life Skills. My love, respect and admiration for him is beyond words. His legacy lives on. As a special treat, I suggest watching a made for T.V. movie about his life. It is called "Unforgivable". The lead part of the life of Paul Hegstrom was played by John Ritter.

SPIRITUAL ARRESTED DEVELOPMENT

In my theory, I do not believe that one can spiritually grow past the age of arrested emotional development until the emotional trauma which has arrested ones emotional growth has been healed and forgiveness given. Whatever age the arrested emotional growth is at in a person, that is as far as the spiritual growth can grow in my opinion. I have witnessed this with client after client in my twenty plus years of observations while teaching Life Skills classes.

If I am arrested in emotional growth at age six years old then spiritually I will only be able to grow toward God at that same rate, pace and understanding as my emotional development will allow me to grow. I cannot understand God at a deeper level until I can understand myself at a deeper level. I need maturity, growth and insight for either of those two things to happen. My emotional age needs to progress toward matching my chronological age to jumpstart my spiritual growth. I must work to heal the traumas of my youth to accomplish this. It takes work but can be done.

A short testimony (of someone I know well), about a man who was once a little boy in a foster home at about age five years old. He and his little sister were in a home together and she was three years old. They were being severely abused in this home and they did not have a way to help themselves or to communicate the problem to someone that would or could help. The little boy wanted to run away and yet every time he would consider doing this he would think about his baby sister who he knew would be left to suffer the abuse alone and he couldn't bring himself to leave her. He told me that he prayed each night that God would help them, but he said his prayers went unanswered. He grew up to be a man who is agnostic and cannot bring himself to forgive God whom he blames for leaving them in that situation when He knew that God had the power to remove them.

This story is so sad because the truth of the matter is that on an Easter Sunday he went to his grandparents with his baby sister for a visit. While there he went to use the bathroom and his aunt who was also visiting happened to walk in while the little boy was using the bathroom and noticed that he had bruises up and down his bottom and legs. She went and got her mother. The grandmother came in and seeing the bruises she immediately called the social services case worker and told them of what they had found. The grandmother on an emergency basis was given immediate custody of the two kids until they could go to court and get a guardianship on them. From the time the two kids were placed in foster care until this was found by the grandmother and the kids were removed was approximately six months.

To children of that age, time takes forever. A week is like a month and for a child to endure the abuse that they did, I am sure that six months seemed like an eternity. In reality, six months was not long when it comes to being in the government system and the prayers of that five-year-old boy were absolutely answered. God heard him and saved them both!

That little boy grew up to be a man that is arrested in emotional development by the trauma that he suffered. His trauma has allowed him to be separated from the God who loves him the most. He will never be able to spiritually grow in God until he is able to heal his emotional wounds and find some resolution and forgiveness for those who abused him. Bottom line is that not only is he emotionally arrested in development, he is equally arrested in spiritual development as well.

Our enemy Satan loves to hurt children. If he can wound their spirit he can separate them from God and that is his ultimate goal. Naturally, we all have in us a belief or feeling of a power bigger than ourselves. Many are taught about his name being God. We learn that God can do anything and when He allows bad things to happen to us we automatically blame Him for allowing it to happen and that causes a division between us and God. Satan belly laughs when that happens because we have never given it a thought that we also have an enemy out there called Satan and that he is the one that is the cause of all evil. God is the deliverer of all that is good.

We must pray against our enemy Satan that he may not wound our children emotionally or spiritually and that God will guard their hearts and minds and protect them from the flaming arrows of the evil one.

The Apostle Paul wrote a verse that reminds me of this subject. 1 Corinthians 13:11 "When I was a child, I talked like a child, I thought like a child, I reasoned like a child. When I became a man, I put the ways of childhood behind me." (NIV)

We can put those issues of childhood away so that we can be mature in Christ, through facing the trauma of our youth with determination to heal.

CHAPTER 6

MIRACLE HEALING

My last big testimony for this book. My prayer is that through the various stories of my life that I have shared, that one of these will resonate with someone enough to make them feel hope for their future.

In January of 2003 I was working as a Director of Nursing. It was hard work. I worked long hours and I was overweight. It seemed that I was growing more and more fatigued and it was all I could do to make myself get up and move. I could not walk very far without getting short of breath. I would have to stop and sit and gather myself and get up and go again. I thought to myself that it was the weight I had gained. I was well over 300 pounds at that time in my life.

One day I was going to a funeral home to try and get things taken care of for a person that I was guardian of that had passed away. There was about five short steps up to where the office was inside. I tried to make it up the steps but could not. Something was wrong and I knew it. I felt very bad and I could not catch my breath. I sat there for a while, by the kindness of the funeral director and then left before doing my business. I had to go to my doctor's office which was just a few blocks away. I went inside and told the lady at the desk what the problem was. They had me sit down and someone came out to take my vital signs. They told me not to move and went to speak with the doctor.

The nurse came out and asked if I thought I could drive or they would call an ambulance but my blood pressure was very high and I needed to go to the hospital immediately. I did not want to pay for an ambulance so I drove myself to the hospital. The emergency room doctor checked me over and did some blood tests. He gave me medications to bring my blood pressure down but would not do anything further. He told me to follow up with my primary care doctor. I left and did not feel much better. With exertion, I continued to be totally out of breath. The doctor did not mention to me that I had liver enzymes up and a hemoglobin that was low. So being the busy nurse that I was, I continued doing what needed to be done for others and put off going to the doctor for myself.

I later had another bout of feeling sick again and ended up back in the emergency room. Same tests, same everything as before only this time the doctor told me that I had anemia and my liver enzymes were up and I needed to follow up with my primary care doctor. This time I did as I was told because I knew that something must be wrong.

I went to see my doctor who was totally amazing. He was calm and simply said he was going to do a sonogram of my liver because of the liver enzymes being so high. He sent me downstairs to have it done. I went back to see him when the results were in and he grabbed my hands and he gently told me that he had some concerns because there appeared to be a tumor on my right kidney. They found it as they were searching my liver for abnormalities. He stated that he was sending me to see a Urologist immediately and that we did not want to mess around with this and that I needed to keep the appointment. Then my wonderful doctor, Chad Schroeder M.D., while holding my hands, began to pray for me. I knew that the report was not going to be good, but his prayers somehow calmed my fear some.

I did not tell anyone yet, as I wanted to know for sure what the deal was that I was facing before I got everyone upset. I kept the appointment and went to see the doctor whom I had worked with at our regional hospital. I knew him to be a good doctor and I knew that he had in the past, had cancer of the kidney as well.

The doctor came in and was so kind and asked if I had anyone with me. I told him that I did not. He sat down with me and gently told me that he had reviewed my sonogram and that it was his opinion that I had renal cell carcinoma which was cancer of the kidney. Hearing those words made me want to scream! I looked out the third story window and it was a beautiful day. I stared at the busyness of the people down on Santa Fe Street and how hurt I felt that the world did not care to stop for just a moment at the sound of my death sentence. To hear the word cancer was bad enough, but to hear renal cell carcinoma was worse because it is a very aggressive cancer. The only person that I knew who had survived it was the doctor that was telling me I had it.

This doctor had navigated this very darkness that he was about to navigate me through. He was very blunt and direct about what needed to be done and how soon. He said that we could not waste time and we needed to get in and take care of it immediately. This was the end of February and I had already wasted time not going to the doctor as I should have. I was so scared. If I died who would take care of my sons? They can't go live with their dad I thought. I began to pray that the Lord would handle things and if I had to die that he not allow it until my kids were eighteen. My youngest was fourteen years old, so I knew I was asking a lot here.

The doctor told me to go home and get my "things in order". Not sure exactly what that meant nor did I want to know. But I knew this was serious. He said I would most likely lose my right kidney completely because of where the tumor was located. He also said that due to the liver enzymes being as high as they were they had decided that they would also biopsy my liver to make sure that I did not have cancer there as well. They would do the biopsy when doing the surgery on my kidney.

Now I had to break it to the family. I let everyone know, even my boys. However, I tried to minimize the issue with the boys so that they would not worry so much. I would be the one to worry. I decided that I needed to make a strategic plan of attack. I needed a miracle and I needed it now. This happened during the time in my life that my faith was the strongest and I knew that either way the outcome, things would be okay. My biggest concern was for my sons. My oldest son was already of age, but he had a one year old which was my first grandbaby and another baby on the way. "Lord" I cried out, "I don't want to miss out on my grandbabies!"

I began to read my Bible and search for any answers that I could find in there. I read a scripture in James 5:14 that said, "Is anyone among you sick? Let them call the elders of the church to pray over them and anoint them with oil in the name of the Lord." So that is exactly what I did first. I went to my pastor and told him of the situation and that I wanted to have the elders pray over me and for him to anoint me with oil which was not normally done in our church. He agreed to do this and after a service on the following Sunday he told the church my situation. He said if anyone wanted to stay over and participate in praying over me as he anointed me with oil that all were welcome.

I sat down and bowed my head and began to pray quietly to myself as others began to lay hands on me and pray. The pastor anointed my forehead with oil and did as the scripture said. I was so surprised when I had opened my eyes and looked around to see that there must have been fifty people that were standing around me praying. I knew in my heart that this was going to work somehow. Satan kept trying to throw me seeds of doubt and tried to keep me in fear, but I just kept trying to find another thing that I needed to do, to divert my attention away from his evil whispers.

I taught Life Skills and I knew that the mind is powerful. God has made us in such a way that we could help Him heal us, or we could help Satan with our impending doom. There is power of life and death in our tongues. It would be my choice of which way I would allow my brain to think. I would repeat scriptures that I knew were truth. When Satan would sling a word of doubt at me, I would sling scripture at him. I would lay in my bed at night and relax and focus on internal healing. I would picture my granddaughter who meant so much to me, as being a little cherub with a bow and arrow. I would then picture her shooting the cancer cells one by one with her arrow and they would blow up and dissolve into tiny little pieces and go into my blood stream to be excreted by my body. I would do this every night. I would pray and pray and then read my Bible over and over searching for answers and hope.

I had to continue to work the best I could while I was waiting for my surgery date. Once my surgical date arrived in March, I went in for the surgery. They had given me the medication to make me groggy and I was giving hugs and kisses to my boys when the nurse came in. They said that the surgery could not go forward due to my lab work returning with my hemoglobin being too low to take the risk. I was devastated because I knew that the longer we had to wait the more risk there was of the cancer spreading. They ran fluids to flush the medications from my system and then sent me home. I had to go the next day back to the hospital to start getting blood transfusions to help raise my hemoglobin level. The cancer feeds off the red blood cells which is why I was having such shortness of breath. The red blood cells carry the oxygen throughout the body and if the red blood cells are low there is less oxygenation in the body.

My surgery would be rescheduled for April 4, 2003. The worry that I was feeling due to anxiety over the cancer possibly spreading was beyond my ability to cope. I kept it to myself to help spare my sons from the worry. Little did I realize that by not talking about things, it only caused them to worry even more. They had no outlet to talk about their fears. In my own fear, I did not think about their fear and how they may have needed to talk about things. I had so much regret about this aspect of my coping or the lack thereof.

My worry was all over my face and I did not realize it. One morning as I was getting ready for work I was tying my shoes when my youngest son turned on some music and jumped out into the living room where I was sitting and began dancing all about the room. He reached down and grabbed his breakaway pants and jerked them off as though he was stripping and pulled his shirt off and there he was dancing in a woman's string bikini! It was hot pink with pink boa feathers across the top and he was ridiculously funny! I stared at this boy in disbelief of what I was seeing and then suddenly I started laughing hysterically. He ran into his room and changed back into his clothes and then came back out and sat on the couch. He smiled big at me. I asked him, "What in the world was that all about at 7:00 in the morning?" He looked me straight in the eyes and said, "Mom, I just wanted to see you smile again." I knew then that we all needed to talk. Every one of us needed to say what we were thinking and how we were feeling. I apologized to the boys for being so caught up in my own fear that I did not consider their fear. We began to talk about things.

I went in for my surgery as scheduled. We as a family all prayed. My pastor, Ron Bowell, came up and prayed with me as well. They did the biopsy of my liver and found that I had benign steatosis of the liver. They ended up removing my right kidney due to the position of the tumor. I went back to the room to recover and as I was waking up from the grogginess of anesthesia I tried to focus on who was in my room but things were blurry. Suddenly my youngest son was up in my face and was shaking a jar all excited and said, "Look mom! I have your kidney! Can I keep it please?" It was a bit shocking to say the least. My sister and brother-in-law both worked in the laboratory at that hospital, so they allowed my son to carry the kidney to the lab. They still needed to dissect it to see if the cancer had busted through the tumor and had gotten into other tissues or not.

I told my son, "I guess you can. I was pretty attached to it. You have to promise to keep it dusted in your room." We have a different type of humor in our family. He was so excited. Everyone had a good laugh.

The lab results came back and it was amazing that it was a stage 2-3 without infiltration. It had remained encapsulated! I would not have to have chemo or radiation! We all praised God for His mercy! While I was in the hospital recouping from my surgery, my boss came to my hospital bed and fired me. She said that the company would no longer need my services. I could not understand how someone could do that with such timing as they did. I had enough to worry about without this happening. But God had seen me through this and I knew He would help me through this additional unexpected storm. Come to find out later through a law suit for unlawful termination, it was discovered that they thought I had cost them too much with health insurance, causing an increase in the group rate. They thought I would be going through chemo and radiation and so they terminated me to prevent further rise in their premiums.

The doctors told me that I would need to have my liver checked annually to monitor that issue because it was a serious one as well. It is a cirrhosis of the liver but not as serious as an alcoholic would have. So, on my annual follow up the next April I went and got my blood work done. The nurse called me back with the results and told me, "I cannot explain it, but your liver function tests are totally normal." I could not believe my ears! I told her, "I can explain it! It was a miracle of God! The Lord made my liver sick so that we would get that sonogram to find the cancer on my kidney! Once we did that He healed my liver! The Lord spared my life on purpose!" I began to cry. The nurse said, "Praise God! I believe you're right. Just keep having the blood work each year to make sure all is well." I told her I would and we hung up the phone.

God's hands were all over this situation. He placed people in my path at the right time when I needed them the most. It was a tag team of people in various events. This very dark time of being fearful of death at the age of forty would not have been something I could have done on my own. The Lord even used a fourteen-year-old teenager to try and make me smile when I felt I had no reason to smile. We learned later that laughter causes the growth of T-Cells which kills off cancer cells. The Bible says in Proverbs 17:22, "A merry heart doeth good like a medicine…" (KJV). Laugh all you can every day. Boost your immune system.

At the time of this writing I am approaching fourteen years of being cancer free! I praise God for the miracle He so willingly gave to me.

Now we will step into the substantive portion of the book that will give you tangible skills that can be very effective if used on a routine basis. A person that is serious about changing their life can make a dramatic difference by using these skills. You can jump start your emotional growth to start catching up with your chronological age, which will allow your spiritual growth to increase as well by using these skills daily. I have seen the change in my own life and the lives of many of my family members. I have seen it happen in hundreds of people that I have taught throughout the past twenty plus years. If you are serious about changing your life, I am serious that you can right here and now. Let's do this!

PART TWO

THE SKILLS

CHAPTER 7

ANGER AND EMOTIONS

Anger is a secondary emotional response to a painful or emotional feeling that we are unable to process or cope with. Anger allows us to maintain a false sense of security in that we believe we can regain control of the situation we are in. However, if we are angry, we absolutely do not have control of the situation or our emotions. In fact, we are very much out of control when we cannot face the emotions that have fueled the fire of the anger we are feeling. We are unable to communicate effectively to the person we are in a struggle with.

Anger will present itself in two basic ways. It will either cause an explosion or an implosion. Either way, anger will make itself known and it can be destructive physically, emotionally, spiritually and mentally. Anger has the power to end relationships that are important to us.

Denial of our responsibility concerning our emotional state keeps us trapped in a cycle of drama. It can only be stopped by our willingness to be accountable for our own behaviors as well as our acceptance of our personal responsibility concerning our emotions. We must be 100% accountable for our behaviors and we cannot use our anger as an excuse for poor behaviors. I will say it again, because it is that important. We are 100% responsible for our behaviors. There is no one that we can blame for the choices that we make, the words that we spew, or the actions that we do. It is 100% on us as individuals.

You can learn to live a more peaceful life if you will be determined and purpose in your heart to do so by taking the first step of the journey. It will not be without work, pain and determination on your part. But if you will put forth the effort it will be worth it in the end.

Imagine if you would, a balloon that has not yet been filled with air. The skin is thick and pliable. There is not much risk that it will break in this state of being uninflated. We will assign one balloon for every situation that may occur in our lives. In each situation that happens we will have some emotions that will arise. These emotions we will place in our balloon and each emotion will have the same effect on the balloon as helium would. The emotions will cause our balloon to grow and grow according to the emotions we are having in each situation. The more situations we have, the more balloons we must manage.

As the balloon grows, its skin begins to stretch and eventually it will grow to its maximum capacity. If we continue to stuff emotions in the balloon past its capacity the balloon will blow-up or pop. When the balloon breaks, it represents that we have hit the point of our anger. Our emotions are the fuel for anger. When we do not deal with emotions while they are less intense, we are fanning the flames of inevitable anger outbursts. When we allow it to go that far, we risk entering the danger zone of implosion or explosion.

Whether I teach a group of patients in the inpatient psychiatric unit or a group of Life Skills students, I will ask them at the beginning of the class for a show of hands of the people that are having an anger problem. I generally will have 3-4 people out of 19 that will raise their hands. I then will ask them to raise their hand if they feel that they have a purpose in life. Generally, only 0-2 will raise their hands. More often than not, no one will raise their hands.

After I have had the show of hands on those two issues I will ask them, "What if I could prove to you that you have an anger problem? Would you consider working hard on the skills that I am about to teach and would you have the courage to admit that you have an anger issue?" They generally will all shake their heads "yes".

I then tell them the story of the balloon. Using the in-patient unit as my example, I will draw a picture of the balloon on the board. I will have each of them tell me some emotions that they were feeling when they were admitted to the behavior health unit. I write down in the balloon each word they say, such as, "fear, hopelessness, sad, depressed, irritable, agitated, hurt, lost, shame, guilt, helpless" to name a few. I will write until I no longer have room in the big balloon to write. I then explain, "When the balloon has stretched to its very limit, it is absolutely going to pop. Do you agree?" They will agree with that analogy.

I will have them reflect a moment and then say, "If our balloon has become so full that it blows up, we know it is because it just cannot handle any more "fuel" which represents our emotions. We also know, that by its popping, it has caused a scenario of either an explosion or an implosion. Is it then a possibility that everyone here may just have an anger issue? Please do not answer yet. I want to continue to prove my point." The class at this point, is at least considering the possibility that they may need to look at their self at least a little bit, rather than the circumstances that brought them into the hospital.

I will begin to discuss the differentiation of implosion vs explosion. I will ask, "What is the worst thing behaviorally that can happen if someone explodes?" Someone will yell out every time, "Homicide". I will say, "correct" and write it on the board at one end of a continuum line. I then ask, "What is the worst thing that could happen behaviorally if someone implodes?" Again, someone will answer, "Suicide". I will say, "that is correct." I will then ask, "How many people here have been admitted because of either feeling suicidal or homicidal?" And nearly 100% of the class will raise their hands. The only ones that do not, are usually people that were admitted by other admission criteria. However, normally everyone in the class will raise their hands. Once they have admitted that they have either exploded or imploded I will ask them, "How many agree that I have proven my point that everyone here has an anger issue and could benefit from learning how to control their emotions, so that their emotions do not control you?" Everyone will then raise their hands with very surprised looks on their faces.

It is a shocking moment when you recognize that you may be the cause of your problems. That is the moment when I must encourage everyone. I let them know that they have a major purpose in life. Homicide and suicide should never be an option. A glimmer of hope is restored by the end of the class and the class is usually willing to do the work.

Have you ever felt this way in your life? I know that I have. I know that the enemy has exploited my emotions and made me feel worthless and unloved. It is a lie. Do not believe it. This is one thing that I cannot tell a class in an institutional setting, but it is the truth and I must tell you. God loves you so much. He does not want you to take your own life or the lives of others. He has great plans for you. He just needs your attention, respect, and obedience. You must be determined enough to never quit and to put to practice what you learn. Be the overcomer, not the victim! You are not too young or too old for God to use you!

In between the implosion and explosion extremes, there are numerous other behaviors and they must be recognized as well. They can serve a warning flags that things are escalating and something needs to cool down and quickly. Familiarize yourself with the things that you do in the in-between stage.

Implosion -- Explosion
Self-mutilation, hitting self, negative self-talk, criticism, yelling, breaking things, hitting others

These are only a few examples of the many other self-destructive and destructive behaviors that can be exhibited by a person who has lost control of their "balloon".

This would be a wonderful time for you the reader to make a list of the behaviors that you have been struggling with yourself. This list is not to make you feel bad about yourself but to start you on the road of empowering you to change the things that you have control over. This is what I call "Controlling the controllable." To do this, we have to be willing to look at ourselves, seriously reflect and recognize the areas that are needing to change in your life. You cannot stop a leak if you do not know where the leak is coming from. Self-evaluation is the beginning of finding the leak so that it can be fixed. Do not fear the evaluation process or feel shame for what you find. It is a time to become excited, because for the first time for many of us we will have true control of a situation that some of us never had control over before!

To recap what we have learned so far:

1. Anger is a secondary emotion to a primary feeling.
2. Anger will happen when we do not manage our emotions.
3. Emotions are the fuel that makes fire causing anger to appear in a situation.
4. Emotions can be managed.
5. Anger will cause either an implosion or explosion.
6. Implosion will cause us to self-destruct.
7. Explosion will cause harm to others and property.
8. The worst thing that can happen when you implode is suicide.

9. The worst thing that can happen with explosion is homicide.
10. Self-evaluation is a must to make significant changes in our lives.
11. We can control the controllable and we can empower our lives to have purpose.

Next, we will begin to look at our specific behaviors a little closer as well as symptoms that happen when we have lost control and have not managed our emotions. Yes, more self-evaluation. We cannot make significant changes in our lives if we do not understand why we do what we do, or how we have lost control over certain aspects of our lives.

BEHAVIORS AND SYMPTOMS

When we live in a constant emotional state, it begins to take its toll on a person. It will affect our spirit by alienating us from God. It will affect our mind by causing internal conflict and torment. It will affect our physical being by increased physical symptoms such as insomnia, anxiety, increased pain, and numerous others. The darkness that we enter can range from mild depression to extreme depression and it can be acute or chronic. This means that if it is acute, it may be caused by a situation that is either unexpected or maybe expected such as a death in the family or loss of a job. We will have to go through the grief and loss process, but eventually we will emerge from that darkness with the right support system in place. It is still painful to experience none the less.

Chronic depression is a deeper realm of darkness that is not as easily worked through. It can be caused by numerous issues such as chemical imbalance that will require medications, or severe childhood trauma that may require psycho-therapy. However, even if we suffer chronic depression we can still take the edge off and maintain some control by controlling that of which we have control, our emotions. Some would argue that if we are chemically imbalanced, a person cannot control their emotions. I would argue that, to a certain degree, a person can maintain control. Even if it is a little bit, we are responsible for our wellness and must try.

Emotions will be expressed and will present themselves in one form or another. It will come out in negative actions/reactions or by physical symptoms within our bodies. Emotions as I have explained in an earlier testimony can cause psycho-somatic death at the extreme end of emotional pain. Rare, but it does and can happen. But what is not rare, when it comes to physical illnesses is that a person can become so focused on physical ailments that they cannot believe that there is a mental issue even involved at all. They become so focused on their physical symptoms that it can become an obsession. You cannot convince someone that is suffering physical ailments that it is all in their head. It is impossible without the correct mental health interventions. They must start getting better through medication and therapy before they can even consider that their emotional pain has caused the physical symptoms. Once they have stabilized with treatment, they can begin the educational classes.

We have grazed over a few behaviors, but we need to look at more detailed behaviors to do a complete exhaustive self-evaluation. Here is a list of behaviors. Read and consider if you have any of these issues or not. If by chance, I have not listed a behavior that you have, maybe something in the list will trigger you to think of something that you may not have thought of otherwise. Repeating some of this information we are going over is to your benefit. Repetition can help us learn things and retain them. I repeat myself some I realize this, but it is to drive the point home because it is that important.

Remember that behaviors come from our inability to cope with our emotions. They can also be produced from a state of Arrested

Emotional Development. When we regress in our emotional age, we will have regressed behaviors that will match our emotional age. If I get upset and I regress to the age of two years old, it is a sure bet that I will do something destructive with my behaviors such as hitting someone or breaking something. We know how a two-year-old will respond when angry. There is a reason it is called the "terrible twos." And like a two-year-old, the only way to change those behaviors in an adult who is arrested in development at that age, is by setting strict limits, boundaries and consequences that are maintained. Otherwise the two-year-old will rule the roost.

We will learn in a little while how to heal the trauma that causes the regressed behaviors. But for now, we are learning to evaluate and assess and recognize the behaviors that we do have. We will learn how to manage a situation in our lives that will ultimately help us to manage our acute emotions which drive our acute behaviors. Now, let us do an honest evaluation of ourselves. Circle the behaviors that you may struggle with or list them on a separate piece of paper. Be real with yourself.

Possible behaviors you may having: Sarcasm, hostile humor, belittling others, critical toward others without love or purpose to encourage positive change, blaming circumstances, blame shifting onto people, gossiping, living with a double standard, hypocrisy, lies, cheats, yells, screams, abusive toward animals, children, elderly or anything that is weaker than you are, misdirect anger toward others, hatred of others, self-loathing, slander, passive-aggressiveness, stealing, self-mutilation, battering others, physical abuse, emotional abuse, mental abuse, selfishness, hoarding, isolating, withdrawing from self, withdrawing from others, anti-social, agitation toward others, breaking things, hitting things, destroying property, making threats to harm self or others, refusing to work, working too much, drinking, drugs, excessive sex, refusal to have sex, spending too much, excessively frugal, gambling, taking high risks, laziness, ignoring the needs of others over your own, judgmental, authoritative, bossy, approval seeker, rigid, compulsive, thrill seeker, dependent, clingy, cynical, over reactor, self-sabotage, procrastination, unable to enjoy fun, unable to follow through, will not keep your word, extremely loyal, unable to maintain personal boundaries for self, invade the boundaries of others, entitlement, no remorse, unable to apologize, super responsible, super irresponsible, set goals so high they cannot be obtained, excessively opinionated, reject others before they can reject you, insecurity, unable to communicate, manipulative, give the silent treatment toward others, easily offended, and unable to give or receive love.

These are just some of the numerous behaviors that can emerge from unhealthy emotions if they are not placed in check. Do not feel bad if you have many of these. The goal is to identify and begin the process to tame these to be manageable behaviors in our lives. We are human and we may never get them all under control completely but even if we were able to get them to be less extreme and less dominate in our lives, it will bring us some real peace. Many times, we create our own chaos and believe it is something or somebody else's' problem, when it is our own. We can get rid of some of these behaviors completely and others we may work on a long time in our lives, but knowing what our issues are will make us accountable to ourselves. If we catch ourselves doing something we know we shouldn't, we can immediately accept responsibility and maybe even apologize to someone sincerely without feeling like we are failures. To apologize does not make us appear weak to others, on the contrary, it makes us look like an adult. We need to feel guilt (not shame), so that we can repent and make a change. No longer do we want to feel shame which makes us feel we are the issue and not the behaviors. I will explain more about this later. Guilt is a warning trigger that we need to take some responsibility.

PHYSICAL SYMPTOMS MANIFESTED

When our emotions control our lives and our stress levels increase, it causes a domino effect in our physical condition. Check the list of possible symptoms and see if you possess any of these. You may think of some that I have not written down. Add them to your list.

Symptoms: Cry a lot, cannot sleep, sleep too much, irritability, fidgety, overly sensitive, fatigued, worry, anxiety, headaches, stomach aches, increased heartburn or gastric reflux, unable to complete a thought, forget things, somatic complaints (symptom focused and constantly complains, some do it for attention), depression, sadness, heart palpitations, chest pain, panic attacks, constipation, diarrhea, all pain will be exacerbated and worse due to stress, uncontrollable muscle twitching, shaking, dizziness, and there are so many more!

Our bodies respond to stress in numerous ways. If we are full of stress then our body will release chemicals to help us deal with the problem. Too much of anything is not good. Cortisol and adrenaline are a couple of the chemicals, as an example, that can be dumped into our system due to, too much stress or fear. These can cause us actual physical ailments and mental problems. If we can control the stress and the emotions we can ultimately control our behavioral and physical symptoms.

So how do we manage our emotions? We will dissect them and learn to control what we are able to control and disregard the rest because it will always shake out. It always does. God has your back. He will take care of what we cannot.

CHAPTER 8

DISSECTING EMOTIONS

HAPPY, SAD OR mad seem to be the most frequently used expression of emotions when describing how we feel. There are so many different emotions that we do not, or are unable to name. There are many varying degrees of intensity of each emotion. Not to be able to understand them leaves us with the inability to appropriately express how we truly feel. It also means we are not able to manage them appropriately. I remember many times in my younger years, when someone would ask me what I was feeling and I did not know how to express what I was feeling. Therefore, I could not express what my needs were. It can leave a person feeling helpless and angrier inside due to being unable to communicate their needs, wants or desires.

Getting some familiarity with emotions and practice recognizing and expressing them will allow us to be able to better articulate our feelings, needs and wants. In this age of high tech and the use of emoticons, it has helped people to identify emotions better. Much translation can be lost in text form, thus the emergence of emoticons to make sure that people understand correctly. However, it does not always work the same with facial expressions from person to person. We can and do misread facial expressions and body language all too often. It can cause an increase in argument. Example: My ex-daughter in law when she gets under terrible stress or devastating circumstances that would cause others to cry, she will laugh. It took me a long time to realize that she was not minimizing the situation, but coping the only way she knew how.

I have always tried to get my students of Life Skills to place emoticons with the emotion names on the refrigerator with magnets if they have children. This will help the kids to start learning at a younger age how to express how and what they feel. It teaches them to identify emotions. It is a great learning tool to have a child pick a face from the refrigerator that best describes how they are feeling. Then have them place the word by that face they have picked and have them say it out loud. "I feel hurt." It cuts down on the tantrums because they can say what they feel rather than act out what they feel. More adults need to learn this process as well. Once the child learns to say how they feel, then we move on to teaching them to identify why they feel that emotion. "I feel hurt because…".

When I learned Life Skills for myself back in the mid 1990's it was such an eye-opening experience for me. It was partially the answer I was seeking. I needed to learn what I was feeling and how to express it appropriately. But what I found was that the classes still lacked something that I needed. I needed to know how to more specifically dissect the emotions I was feeling in order to control them, so they did not control me. Learning to recognize my emotions was huge for me. I needed to learn that skill there is no doubt, but I needed to know more. It took me a while to figure out what I was missing, but I knew something was still not complete for me. In fact, it took me helping others figure it out in a classroom setting before I realized exactly the step that I was missing for myself. I needed to be so intimate with my emotions that I could dissect them and place them in their proper place so that I could control them. This ultimately gave me the blessing of self-control in this area of my life that I did not have before.

Now I am not saying that I have perfect self-control. I do not. I do however, handle myself much better than I did twenty years ago. I at least have the skills to accept constructive criticism when I need to be put into check with my behaviors. I can then re-adjust them immediately. I do still struggle with criticism that comes from people who do not love me or are delivering the information in a non-loving way. Especially if they are pointing out my shortcomings with the wrong motive in their heart. I am human and can still get defensive in that particular situation. When approached in a gentle loving manner, I can receive.

Remember that big balloon of anger that was filling up with so many emotions? Now it is your time to learn how to deal with the emotions that you are feeling or avoiding by stuffing them away. Emotions that are overwhelming you, will fill your balloon full to maximum capacity. They will pump it so full of dangerous fuel, it can ignite either an explosion or implosion. Either way, it will harm you and those whom you love and ruin relationships. With implosion, we may harm ourselves. With an explosion, we may harm others. Neither one is a good thing as we all know.

If we will begin to dissect our emotions and face them head on when we first start feeling them, we can diffuse the anger before it ever escalates. If we do not pay attention to what we are feeling and bury our heads into the sand because we do not want to deal with the situation, then we can rest assured that the explosion or implosion will come. We will deal with it sooner or later but at a much greater risk to the things that we say are important to us.

When I first started teaching how to dissect emotions, I would have the student fill a paper balloon with written emotions concerning a hot topic in their lives. I would then have them take every single emotion that they wrote down and put them in order of priority of how much distress it was causing them and place them in a column. Then with each word, they were to go down and answer the question, "Why am I feeling this?" They had to say why they felt that one emotion. Then they had to answer another follow up question. Whatever was written down as the reason for that one emotion, they had to answer, "In this situation what do I have actual control over?" This began the journey of controlling the controllable. But as we practiced this long and daunting task that seemed never ending, our balloons were stuffed with emotions and it took forever to dissect them. Though it was good practice, it did not take long to realize that no one would take the time to do this. Then I recognized a common denominator in the listed emotions that everyone was writing and even myself when I did the exercise with them. **FEAR** was in the top ten of every list that I looked at. In fact, it appeared to be the number one answer.

I decided to see what would happen if I dissected the emotion of fear first. As I answered the questions for this one emotion it became clear that fear was the author of all the other negative emotions that I was feeling. I realized that if I was to get resolution with my fear first that it would immediately decrease the intensity, dissipate and often eradicate all of the other emotions I was struggling with in that situation. The best way to teach you how to do this skill is to give you an example to follow that you can use as a step by step directions that you can refer to again for other situations.

Example/Situation: A man named John and his wife have three kids. John lost his job and turned to doing drugs to cope. The wife fed up with the situation, the constant fighting over their daily survival and John's lack of work or willingness to work, as well as his using drugs to cope with life, she decided to take the kids and go to her mother's home. The man received an eviction notice and now there is seemingly zero hope to restore his family because he doesn't even have a home to bring the family back to. He ends up homeless, on the streets, surviving one day at a time in the most disgusting of situations. He feels he has no control over anything in his life. He considers committing suicide to end this nightmare. He believes that everyone would be better off with him dead. All seems hopeless. He is overwhelmed with so many emotions that he cannot handle them and he begins the process of imploding. He sees no light at the end of the tunnel. All is dark

Step #1: John must look at his balloon. What are the emotions that he can recognize? He will need to start to write them down. What you put down on paper is no longer overwhelming in your head, so get it out of there! It is a step in taking control of a dire situation. Some of the emotions may be as follows: depressed, sad, scared, hopeless, helpless, worthless, fearful, self-loathing, demoralized, lonely, alienated, miserable, and no doubt the list can go on and on in this situation.

Step #2: Identify why you feel each emotion. When you make the list of why you feel each emotion, what you will find is that you have now made a list of the things that are causing you to feel overwhelmed. This is the list that you will begin to start making an action plan from, so that you can gain back control over your life. List and cluster the emotions that have similar likeness in meaning. Even though we may feel these emotions, if we can cut them down to size by their meaning. it will be one more step in decreasing the feeling of being overwhelmed. The racing thoughts that float in our heads can crush our spirit and paralyze us from acting. I have placed the emotions of feeling scared and fearful purposely at the bottom of the list. It is to demonstrate how one step different will help you do this exercise faster. But for the sake of learning the process, we will do it long form for now. We have identified our emotion list and clustered the ones that are like one another.

1. Depressed, Sad
2. Hopeless, helpless
3. Worthless, self-loathing, demoralized
4. lonely, alienated
5. miserable
6. Scared, fearful

Now we will reflect on each cluster and answer the question of **"Why?"**

1. I feel depressed and sad because: **I have lost everything, my job, my family, my home, my integrity, my dignity. I am embarrassed and humiliated as well.**
2. I feel hopeless and helpless because: **I do not know what to do to stop the losses. I do not know what to do to fix it all. I do not see an end in sight. I feel suicidal because I am worthless and my family would be better off without me anyway.**
3. I feel worthless, self-loathing and demoralized because: **I failed. I cannot do anything right. I caused everything to fail and I hurt my family. It is all my fault.**
4. I feel lonely and alienated because: **I lost my wife and kids. My family is not helping me. My friends have pulled back from me and I have no one. Yes, I have isolated myself. I feel so foolish and such a failure, but if they cared they would come to me.**

5. I feel miserable because: **I have created such a mess! I am alone, I miss my family, I want to work and have my own home, I really do not want to die but I see no alternative. I hate what my life has become. I hate who I have become.**
6. I feel scared and **FEARFUL** because:
   a. I have lost everything, my job, my family, my home, my integrity, and self-respect. I want my family back but I don't think it will ever happen.
   b. I don't know how to stop the losses. I do not know how to fix things and make them right again.
   c. I am a failure. I have caused this mess.
   d. I am all alone in this and it is scary. I wish I had someone who cared.
   e. Suicide has become an option for me and I do not want to die but it seems that it is the only answer right now.
   f. I want my old life back and I do not think it will ever happen.
   g. I have lost who I am. I do not even know the person I have become. If I admit that to anyone, I will be seen as a weak person. I have admitted that I am a failure and it is all my fault. Who could possibly love a failure?
   h. I am afraid that my family will never forgive me. Why would they? I cannot forgive myself.

Notice that what the man was feeling with every other emotion at the top of his list was the same thing that fear was causing him to feel as well. I now start with fear first each time I dissect emotion because it shortens down the steps in this process of dissection of emotions.

In this self-evaluation, there are many things are at play here. Before we go to the next step I just want to point out the variables that are influencing the thoughts of this young man.

1. **Negative self-talk:** The things that we tell ourselves that are negative and we believe them because they are life commandments. It is difficult to change our belief system without reprogramming our sub-conscience mind to believe truth. We have believed the lies that we have learned throughout our lives. It can be done. We can learn to dissect emotions. We can reprogram our thinking. We will always be at an internal war with ourselves until we change the way our mind thinks and processes things.
2. **Perception:** His perception causes him to believe that others could never care for him because of what he had done. He believes that he is unforgiveable. He is unable to separate who he is from what he has done. He feels great shame. Shame says that we are what we have done. We cannot change that thought process without changing the programming in our subconscious mind. We must face the demons of our past. What are the wounds that need to be healed? He believes himself to be a failure. It will not change until his perception of himself changes.
3. **Being the Victim:** What is the secondary gain for this person to remain a victim of circumstance? Sometimes it is easier to make excuses for the position we have gotten ourselves into and remain in hopelessness. We are not expected to rise above the circumstances when others have given up on us or we have given up on ourselves. It takes work to heal. Let's face it, some people have become so dependent upon others to do the work for them, that it is just easier to

remain in the gutter. Maybe this guy has "friends" giving him free food, a couch to flop on and allows him to remain responsibility free. Who would want to give that up? It is a secondary gain. He does not have to be held accountable to the things that he has done in this situation. It is not comfortable to be held accountable by others. It is much easier to bask in self condemnation than to be condemned by others. Even if what others are saying is not actual condemnation, it is perceived to be by the "victim". Ah, that perception thing again! Don't forget that if someone truly wants to be a victim, they will blame you for the problem and never accept responsibility in their part no matter how small their part may have been.

We will address these three things as well in a little bit. If we do not heal the inside trauma, we will simply go through the motion of doing skills to change things. We will not get to the root cause of the problem. It will be like using a band-aide on a gaping wound. We leave room for self-sabotage, because inside our hearts, we will be in an internal conflict between truth and lies. We will know that the skills are a truth, but we will not believe the truth concerning the value of who we are as a human being. We will believe the lies that are programmed in our minds. For true victory, we must exchange the lies for truth. The best place to discover our value is in the ultimate Truth, God's Word, the Holy Bible. As our creator, He knows who we are best.

Step #3: As you can see from our list of emotions that **FEAR** covers the worries and beliefs of all the other emotions. Fear trumps them all! What I discovered is that for every situation we have, we carry a balloon with thousands of various emotions. The more situations I have, the more balloons I have. The more balloons I have, the more emotions I have. The more emotions I have, the more chaos rules my life. Every balloon has one common emotion that is shared between them. It is called FEAR. If we will dissect just the fear emotion alone in each balloon, it will dissipate all the other emotions and prevent an implosion or explosion of anger. Allow me to prove this to you.

Now that we have a long list of things that we are fearful of, we must search through the list to make an action plan of the things we can control. Not everything can be controlled by us. Those things which cannot be controlled will eventually lose their power over us. What we focus on gains power.

We must focus on the list of things that we can control. Good or bad, whatever we focus on becomes bigger! It can consume us. Which would you rather be consumed by? The things that are controllable or the things that are not controllable? Let's make the controllable things in our life the focus and make them huge! Victory is on the way!

ACTION PLAN: An action plan is putting plan to paper. It once again takes things out of the head and puts them in a visual form. We can begin to make the problem manageable. This will allow you to sleep at night because all the worries are now being placed in a controlled environment. You are taking steps to change things one problem at a time. You are now in control of the situation.

In the action plan, we are isolating the problem that needs to be solved. We are using the dissection of the emotions that we identified. You will then transfer the problem to the action sheet and begin to list action steps to solve the problem. It may take several steps to solve some problems and it may only take one or two steps to solve another. Writing the steps down will help you to put things into perspective. It will allow you to mark things off your list as you accomplish them. It gives you a daily victory toward your goal of fixing the problem! It will encourage you to keep your focus real and where it needs to be daily. So, let's begin.

On a piece of paper write categories that look something like this:

ACTION PLAN

PROBLEM	**STEPS TO ACTION**	**TARGET DATE**
Job loss	Put out 5 applications a week every week.	Now.
Using drugs to cope	Enter outpatient drug rehab, join Celebrate Recovery.	3/2
Homeless	Save money once I start working for rent/deposit.	4/1
Loneliness	Surround myself with positive people. Find a church.	3/5

The action plan addressed the practical things that need to be done, to begin changing the situation. If the person will focus on just these things and not on the variables, these things will be taken care. Like a domino effect, it will knock out all the other issues that once were beyond our control. Fear will dissipate. Maybe the wife who sees that John is trying hard to make things change, will learn to admire his effort and begin to respect him again (Women will not invest into a man she cannot or does not respect.). She may even step up beside him as his friend. Maybe their friendship will begin to grow. When she sees that he is serious about sticking to the plan, she can learn to trust him again. She may start to believe that he will be responsible to care for his family once again. She might take the chance on reconciliation with John. But, how will John ever know if he does not do his part? He won't.

There are instances that reconciliation does not happen no matter how hard you try. However, you will never know unless you try. And should reconciliation not be in the future for you, there is still a brighter future ahead of you. If you stick to the plan you have laid out, positive things will happen for you. Allow for the possibility of a brighter future simply because you are making better choices. We all make bad choices from time to time. We must learn to recognize them and stop the self-condemnation. Forgive yourself. Learn to control the controllable. Move forward.

Let's do a **recap summary** of what we have learned here.

1. List the emotions that are overwhelming you.
2. Prioritize them placing fear first.
3. List what you are fearing concerning the situation. Do not leave anything out.
4. From your list of fears pick out the things that you know you have some potential ability to control. Do not sell yourself short.
5. Build an ACTION PLAN. You can make it as detailed as you need to do in the action steps. (The one that I did was simple and basic in order to give you an example.)
6. Implement your action plan and do not stop until you have gained victory.
7. Do not allow the variables to distract you. Focus on the controllable things.

You are on your way to changing things in your life for the better. Never give up. Readjust things on your action plan if things change. Nothing is set in stone.

VERTICAL VS HORIZONTAL THINKING

One last thought on this area I want to share. When I was teaching Life Skills in the mid 1990's I was so excited to help others. I would sometimes be discouraged that I had only 10 to 15 people in a classroom. I wanted to help an auditorium filled room with people because I could see the value of the things that had helped me heal my life. I wanted to share it all with others. I wanted to mass produce the help for others and was discouraged when I lacked the ability to do it.

The Lord knew my heart and loved that I wanted to help others. He gently spoke to me and told me that I was viewing things wrong. "What?! Whatever do you mean Lord? How could my wanting to help millions rather than 15 people possibly be viewing things wrong?" It did not take but a minute for the Lord to set me straight. He told me, "You are viewing things horizontally when you should be viewing them vertically". It made no sense to me. He said that He was the Lord of all things. It is His job to see the big picture. He places people where they need to be to make sure that everything works out to the good of His glory. It was my job to do what He has asked me to do and do my part well. When I do my part well, I am contributing to the big picture and eventually I will see it.

He then asked me, "Are not the 15 people that I have placed in your classroom important enough for you to help?" I said, "Yes! Yes, they are! I never meant to infer that they were not." I then felt guilty for not considering those that I was helping as being important, because they were very important.

Yet, still that was not the point that God wanted me to take away from this conversation of thinking vertically. He told me that not all harvest is done like a microwave with instant gratification. Sometimes it comes slowly over time. True transformations take time, energy and effort. He wanted me to realize that if I would think vertically and be patient that my small crop would eventually yield thousands! "How Lord? How will my 15 people yield thousands?" I simply could not see that. I was too busy trying to see the big picture that I could not focus on the little plot of fertile ground that I was planting. I only had 15 seeds that I was planting. What could that produce I wondered.

The Lord then showed me. He asked how many children each person in my class had. At that time, I believe that there were around 25 total kids that would be off-spring to the people that I was teaching in my class. He then asked how many had either spouses or girlfriends. I believe that there was 12 or 13 at that time. The Lord then asked me if I thought that those I was teaching would benefit from the curriculum? And I had to say that they were. He then asked, "If people would benefit from the program, wouldn't they want to share it as passionately as you have?". Ouch! I thought wow, He has made a very good point. He then asked me how many people out of my class would directly or indirectly benefit from this information that I was sharing. I had to humbly respond by saying at least 53. This number grew from the 15 directly affected in class that I could physically see. Those at home that were being indirectly affected by what the class was learning by the changes being made in the people taking the class. However, their behavior changes were directly affecting and influencing those around them in their homes.

The Lord did not stop there with me. He then stated, "You are now planting seeds in 53 people. What happens if those people go on to share with others what they have learned? What if the changes in their lives became a new way of life to them and those around them? What if they had children or even grand-children? How many people could possibly be affected by the little class that you were teaching?" He then reminded me that I was wanting to horizontally teach thousands of people, when he was calling me to teach vertically to thousands of people. It became apparent to me that sometimes we get into a pattern of thinking that does not allow us to grow ourselves. I then became more excited about my little plot of land that the Lord had given me to plant seeds in. The "big picture" is for the Contractor to view, or in this case the Creator. I realized that the big picture only sees the surface of things, it does not show the depth. We must think vertically to recognize the depth of what we are called to do. God sees both.

Do not be discouraged as you focus on your little steps to do. They can have major impact in the big scheme of things. Never give up. Press on toward the goal one step at a time. Think vertically and go deep! Dig into your action plan and change your little plot of ground dramatically! As for me, I pray at least 15 people read this book!

CHAPTER 9

GARBAGE IN, GARBAGE OUT

THE SUBCONSCIOUS MIND is like a computer. Many say that it is a filtering system for all that we say and do, because it influences our decisions. I have learned that it is not only a filtering system, but it is a data base that stores things. When we receive messages, the information that is stored inside becomes solidified as our belief system.

Where do these messages come from? They are deposited by those that love us. The messages make the most impact when we love and respect those that are making the deposit within us. Babies are born with a clean slate. They do not have a bunch of garbage that has been stored in their data base and they do not have an established belief system. Their perceptions are not yet hampered or tainted by the sad things of this world that eventually become part of their data base as they grow up.

In life skills, the negative and positive messages that is deposited into our subconscious data base becomes what is called **Life Commandments**. This phrase was coined by Dr. Tim Savage who was a professor of the neurobiology of the brain. He taught neurolinguistics which is another fascinating subject of how we communicate. Neurolinguistics teaches, if people do not bridge to the proper communication mode of another person it can cause conflict. On the other hand, if we do connect properly to the other person's mode of communication, we can communicate not only effectively but restore relationships.

LIFE COMMANDMENTS

So, what is a life commandment? It is the data received into our subconscious minds that becomes embedded and eventually becomes our truth. Words, sayings and even actions of those we love, especially our parents are deposited within us. We learn to believe it. It becomes ingrained as our belief system. Some examples of **negative life commandments** that we would want to change are:

1. You will never amount to anything.
2. You are just like your mother/father.
3. You are ugly.
4. You are fat.
5. You are unloved.
6. You are useless.
7. What is wrong with you? (Inferring a message that something is wrong with you.)
8. You are a jerk.
9. You are stupid.
10. I have never seen anything like you. (Inferring that you are the worst thing ever seen.)

These are only to name a select few. This is the "garbage in" messaging that we begin to insert into a child's mind, when in our frustration, we do not choose our words carefully while correcting them. It is poisonous venom and it will only serve to cause there to be "garbage out" eventually. It will manifest itself in poor attitudes, poor behaviors, miscommunications and a life time of difficult relationships to name a few. It will skew our perceptions to the point that everything that someone says will become an inferred message and we will be easily offended. Once offended then we will no longer hear what the messenger's true intent was, because we have heard enough. The emotional pain will not allow us to receive anything more. Overload!

People that are wounded in this way will self-sabotage and they will never be happy, no matter what the spouse, friend or child may try to do to make them. They will not be able to receive or to give love. The wounded person will not even understand the truth of what love really is because of their misperception that has already been given to them. Their life commandments will prevent them from knowing the truth. The ultimate assault upon the person who is wounded by the life commandments is; because God IS love, they will not be able to approach the very throne of God that can heal them here and now. Changing the data base is critical to healing our lives.

SHAME VS GUILT IN DEPTH

People who have received this negative garbage become **shame based** in their thinking. God has made a perfect plan for our lives and given us instruction of how to live it. Satan has a perfect mirror image of everything God has. He masks it to look deceptively like what God has laid out, but it is not. God set us up to feel guilty when we have done or said something that we know was wrong. Guilt is a small trigger or nudge telling us, "Hey, you shouldn't have done that. Apologize and make it right." We with a good subconscious mind will do just that. We will recognize the error and repent from it and make it right the best that we can immediately. We can let it go after that and move on never giving it another thought. There is no condemnation from God or from ourselves, especially if we are in Christ Jesus.

Satan on the other hand, wants a child to be wounded and receive negative life commandments generously. It is so that he can inflict his version or form of guilt upon us, which is called shame. Shame makes us feel that we are the sin or the terrible things that we have done. We cannot separate who we are, from what we have done. If someone criticizes us constructively, even if done in total love, we will be offended. Because the criticism will appear as a personal attack against us and not the behaviors that are being subject to accountability. If we already have feelings of self-condemnation, then we are set up to feel even more condemned by anyone that might have what we perceive as a negative word against us. No matter how gentle or diplomatic the words that are spoken for constructive criticism are, they no doubt will be rejected.

Guilt allows us to know that when we are called into accountability that it is not us, as a person being called out but the behaviors that we have done. We can accept responsibility and we can correct the problem. We can have remorse and we can apologize sincerely. The issue is easily placed in the past and many times never to be recalled again.

Shame makes us know in our heart that when we are called into accountability that it is a personal attack because they obviously hate us. We cannot accept responsibility and we will never apologize because to do so means that we admit that we are the scum of the earth. We may feel remorse inside of us and it will only fuel more negative self-talk that will then bear witness to the already negative life commandments that we possess. It will be stored in our mind for reuse repeatedly. A constant reminder that we not any good. Which by the way, is a lie.

PERCEPTION

All these things combined give us a negative perception. Our perception is the filtering system we have developed from the life commandments that have been deposited. Someone may say something good but then we may perceive that they meant something bad or had a hidden message or motive to what they were saying. We will lack trust in most everyone that says something that is contrary to what we have learned to believe about ourselves. We will believe that there must be an ulterior motive to why they would say something good about us. After all, we know how bad we really are. We know that no one could love someone like us. And if they did, they must have something wrong with them. This is a set up for a play pen disaster in any relationship. The term "play pen" is my way of saying two adults are engaging into childlike behaviors.

When a person feels this way about people in their lives, then imagine how they may feel about having God in their lives! It only causes feelings of more shame and embarrassment. The Bible is full of love and wonderful things that our Creator believes and feels about us. If Satan has wounded our spirit to the point of being so shame filled that we cannot allow any person to love us, how can we approach a Holy God? First, we will not believe that God could or would think such positive things about us. Even if we could swallow the possibility that He may love us we simply will feel that we must change first before we present ourselves to Him. We will reject His love if we feel self-condemnation because we will not feel worthy enough to receive it. Our enemy has fooled us to believe that we must change first, when the truth is, our transformation begins once we accept God!

VICTIM VS VICTOR

I have already given numerous examples of how people can perceive themselves to be a victim in any given situation. I shared my own testimony of my struggles being a victim. I wanted to briefly state that if we feel that we are receiving more attention from people by being a victim, there is no incentive to learn to be victorious. Even negative attention is more valuable than no attention at all. So, if I cannot get your attention by being healthy and happy, then I will get your attention by becoming somatic and sickly. Everyone needs attention to some degree. Some feel that they need it more than others and will rival anyone that tries to take what they feel belongs to them, even unjustly so.

This is a bad set up for sibling rivalry when a parent will compare one child with another. One child is perceived as the bad child and the other is perceived as the good child. Both will feel that they were neglected by their parents. The "bad" child will feel that the good child got all the attention and was loved more. The "good" child will feel that the other one got more attention due to them being bad all the time. In a step-parent situation, it can cause the step-parent to rival their step-kids for attention and love from their spouse and vice versa. This can destroy a family quickly.

Learning to love yourself is the answer. You cannot receive or give what you do not have. It does not matter if you spent eight hours a day with the person that is wounded. It will never be enough. They will always need that five minutes more and all would have been well. This is a lie we tell ourselves. You cannot do enough favors for the wounded person, it will never be enough to prove you love them. Until a person is sick of being the victim, they will not change.

FORGIVENESS

Part of giving up being a victim is learning forgiveness. This is a double-edged sword. When we are wounded, and are full of negative life commandments, stuck on being the victim we can neither receive nor give forgiveness. It is like receiving and giving love. Neither one is possible if we are stuck in the wounds of our past. We cannot give what we do not have, and we cannot receive what we fear. We must evaluate and decide if the secondary gain of being a victim is better than what we may gain once we are to become a victorious survivor of our past. We can become a prosperous light in a very dark world. To be a light, generates for us a purpose in our lives. We all need a purpose to survive. We need to be needed. We need to be loved. We were created to love and to be loved.

Forgiveness is a decision. Forgiveness is not an emotional response, though it may be emotions that bring us to the point of decision. We may even feel emotional about the situation. However, the Lord says in His Word that for us to be forgiven by Him we must be willing to forgive others. How unfair of us it would be, if we demanded that God forgive us of our sins and wrong doings and yet we would deny forgiveness to others for theirs. Who are we to receive what we feel others are not entitled to receive?

There is an old saying I have used many times, "Unforgiveness is like me drinking poison waiting for you to die." The other person does not need to know that you have forgiven them for you to forgive. Example: If your parent hurt you badly but they have died. You do not need to be able to tell them personally that you forgave them. To be obedient to God about forgiving them, you must simply make the choice to forgive them and proclaim that to the Lord. Your healing will emerge as a small light and in time will be a torch for all to see! It affects how we act and respond toward others. If we are forgiving and loving it will shine in our faces. If we are unforgiving and unloving, it too will also show in our faces.

In one of my situations at age 8-years-old, I was a molested. I did not tell my molester that I had forgiven him when I was finally able to do it. I simply made the decision and told God and asked

Him to help me through the emotions of it all. For me it was about submitting my healing needs to God. It was about no longer allowing the molester to take up room in my head rent free. It was about not allowing my molester to continue to control my life thirty plus years later in all that I said and did. It was about releasing myself from bondage so that I would no longer be the victim. I could now victoriously walk in the light and leave the shame behind and help others navigate the darkness of this area. It gave my life purpose and meaning. It set me free.

I kept that secret locked away inside of myself until I was 32-years-old. I am here to tell you that secrets keep you sick. They torment your mind. Find someone that you trust and share with them the pain of your heart and the thoughts of your mind. I was held in bondage until I could speak the truth. It was getting it out that set my feet upon a path of healing that wound.

Now is the time for you to set yourself free. Give forgiveness and accept forgiveness. Accept forgiveness by the one true God that can change everything for you in your life. "For all have sinned and fallen short of the glory of God." We all need a Savior and Jesus paid our debt. We only need to accept his gift by holding ourselves accountable, accepting responsibility for our sins and handing them over to Him so that He may stamp them "Paid in Full"!

What a feeling of relief and a stripping away of all the shame. Jesus differentiates the difference between who we are and what we do. He is interested in who we are and He paid the debt for what we did. Yes, it is another decision to be made. The choice is yours. Sometimes our decisions are the hardest thing to do based on our own stubbornness and pride. If you believe that Jesus died and rose from the grave and you are willing to confess it with your mouth. You will overcome the world and can look forward to a future life of eternity full of "son-shine" and happiness! For Jesus is the light of the world!

BREAKING THE LIFE COMMANDMENTS SKILL:

Well, I bet you thought I had forgotten to tell you how to fix this situation huh? Nope! I just needed to show you how much garbage comes from these lies we embed into our brains. I needed you to see the damage that it causes. I needed you to see how you might identify with some of this junk for you to see the necessity in doing this skill.

It is a simple skill. It is one of the most important and impactful skills that you will do for yourself. In fact, if you will do this skill for your children, you will change their world and be possibly the best parent that ever was!

If garbage can be inputted by words, then it can be deleted by words. Now the fact that we have had negative words embedded into our subconscious mind, for some of us many years, means that we need to be diligent in using words daily to undo the damage done. We need to interject positive words and they need to be powerful. All words are powerful but some are more powerful than others. Words that hold truth will set you free! The Lord said that there is power of life and death in the tongue. Speak life!

STEP #1:

Make a list of the things that you tell yourself under your breath in times of stress that are negative. Most likely they will end up being the very words you were told by someone that said that they loved you. The person most likely did love you, but due to their own dysfunctional life they did the best they could with the skills that they had. So, forgive them! Write down every negative thing that you feel about yourself. It may be a lengthy list, but that is okay we want to get that stuff out. "Better out than in!" as quoted by Shrek. ☺

STEP #2:

Take the top ten things that hurt you the most on that list and then write ten positive truths to counteract those venomous lies. Example: "I am unloved" and "I have no worth". You can simply say the opposite, "I am loved" and "I am valuable". However, sometimes it is hard to convince ourselves if we do not have something as proof that this is truth. I like to use scripture. I know it is God's Word and I know it is true. I always thought it was truth for others and not for me but over a time of healing I realized that it was absolutely for me too! I use them for my grandchildren too, as I have told you already. Here is a good list to start the positive self-talk with if you need help.

1. I am loved by God.
2. I am the righteousness of God through Christ
3. I can do all things through Christ who strengthens me
4. I am fearfully and wonderfully made
5. God has a purpose for my life
6. I am chosen by God
7. I have a destiny
8. I can love and be loved
9. I can forgive and be forgiven
10. I am valuable and worthy to be loved

STEP #3:

Now you will type or write these on two pieces of paper. Tape one on the mirror that you use every day to prepare for your day and place one by the toilet paper roll on the wall.

You will begin to speak these powerful words into truth. These words will delete the old data and replace it with these new truths that you have listed. You must speak the words out loud for your subconscious mind to hear your voice. It is your voice that your subconscious mind will believe over all others. You need to speak these out loud twice a day. Once in the morning to start your day out positive. Then once before bed so that when you go to sleep your mind will retrieve and assimilate what you have imputed into the subconscious mind to be stored.

Let me tell you that this will be very uncomfortable at first when you start doing it. The reason is that the list is going against our current belief system. You won't believe what you are saying at first. It is going against all you have believed yourself to be. You are retraining your mind to believe something else. It is called the truth. No longer will we believe the lies of Satan. He will fight you on this.

I have learned through my experience and excuses from others, that there is just not enough time in the day to fit these ten sentences into our busy schedules. Alas! That is why I strategically placed these sentences in two places where multi-tasking can be done. While you brush your hair, put on make-up, shave or brush your teeth in the morning speak these words into life! While you are using the toilet at night (or any other time of day), speak these words into existence! There is no excuse as to why they cannot be done in less than one minute.

Each day these sentences of truth will become easier to say. Then you will begin to realize that it is becoming your truth and your new belief system. New attitudes will arise. You will begin to show love and accept love. You will learn to give grace and mercy to others that you never could before. As the saying goes, "The deeper the pain, the higher the expectations we have". Our expectations for ourselves and others will be more normalized as we heal. Some people have so much pain that Jesus Christ Himself could not jump over their expectations. As we learn to love ourselves, our expectations will become reasonable for ourselves and for others.

We will begin to forgive others for their failures before they even realize that they need forgiveness. We may have more desire to receive forgiveness from others, whereas before we may not have cared. We will be able to accept responsibility for our actions and not fear being held accountable to them. We will learn that fights will end when we can simply accept ownership of our part and apologize for it. Life will not be perfect, but it will sure feel less stressed and chaotic. We will feel a sense of peace we never felt before. It means that healing is in progress.

Transformation is a process. It takes time. Do not be hard on yourself, but do be diligent to do the work needed to make the transformation process work. I have not arrived yet, myself. Every day I have a new area that God says He wants me to grow and expand in. It took me seven years to get this book done. Because of my lack of obedience, life got hard. I made every excuse there was as to why I was not the person to write this book. The Lord made sure that I learned the hard way that "God does not call the qualified, but he qualifies the called". He allowed me to suffer natural consequences of my actions and decisions without any buffer. He did this so that I would learn and I would "pick it up" and run with the task that he gave me. He wanted me to simply obey without questioning Him or His motives. Trust and obey. These are difficult lessons in life.

CHAPTER 10

EMERGING AS LIGHT

"And they overcame him by the blood of the lamb, and by the word of their testimony; and they loved not their lives unto the death."

Revelation 12:11

There are many problems in this world. Most of them originate with people. Hurting people will hurt people. Our enemy knows this. He can benefit greatly by harming young children by wounding their spirits. His plan is to prevent the healing that is needed to reconcile their lives with the Lord Jesus Christ. The scripture that I have written above is powerful. It tells us that there are two very strategic and commanding ways to overthrow our enemy. By the blood of the lamb who is Jesus Christ, and by the word of their testimony which is us telling our stories! You have a testimony waiting to be heard by someone!

WORD OF OUR TESTIMONY

Our testimony comes from our war zones. They come from the battles that we have won and the battles we have lost. It is the scars that we have endured, the pain we have suffered and the hope that we have gained from navigating the darkness and emerging as light, that gives us purpose.

Our testimonies can give hope to a dying and divided world. When we share the things that are good that can come from tragedy through our own experiences, it offers hope and encouragement. Where there is hope, there are possibilities. Speaking out about what we have gone through in life, not only brings hope to others, it brings personal healing to ourselves. Our words are containers full of power, light and life if we choose positive words to speak. The words we speak that are negative are equally powerful and can destroy life. The Lord says that there is power of life and death in the tongue as I have already said. Choose life! Yes! Another decision. The more we speak of our life tragedies, the more distant the pain becomes. It begins to feel like you're removed from the situation and it becomes a story. Your story. Your testimony. Tell it.

You may be suffering in pain right now. You may be lonely, sad and depressed. You may not have any hope left in you. I am here to tell you that you will get through this time of despair. Your life has meaning. The lessons that you are learning in daily life will help you find your purpose. You will first be navigated through your hardships and then you will learn to become the navigator for someone else. You cannot not allow bitterness and resentment to chain you to the enemy. You will overcome this with the blood of the lamb and eventually the word of your testimony! The decision is yours of course.

THE BLOOD OF THE LAMB

In my life, I have suffered many losses. Though I have shared some of the things that I have gone through, there are so many more that I could have shared and did not. This I can tell you, without a doubt, I could have been so bitter and resentful. Believe me, there was a time in my life that I was, but life is too short to live that way.

That is one lesson I wish I had learned sooner in my life. When I did finally learn that lesson, it was then that I began to have a very real and close personal relationship with God. The closer I drew toward Him, the closer He drew to me. God is a gentleman and will not push Himself upon you. Relationship takes effort. If we will not crack open a Bible, we obviously do not value the relationship we could have with God. He speaks to us through the Bible. We cannot hear his Word if we do not enter His Bible and relate with Him.

When I searched for Him with all my heart and mind, that is when my life began to really change. Yes, these basic skills can help a person all by themselves to some degree without bringing God into the equation. But why have something just good, when you can have something that is great! It is like eating a meal without spices, bland and humdrum. I always had a void that was not filled. It lacked something that I was not able to identify. I came to the realization that I needed God in my life to oversee me. I had to do it through Jesus, who paid the debt for my natural sin and the sins that I made an obvious choice to do on my own. I just had to be humble enough to say that without Him I cannot make it. Without Him I am lost. Without Him I had no hope. He is the keeper of the flame, the light of the world. He gave me the light to which I have emerged from the darkness. Thank you, Jesus!

I always had a sense of emptiness on this journey we call life. I rarely shared that with anyone. When I was not connected to the power source of light, I had zero hope. There was nothing that this world had to offer me that could fill my void. Drugs, food, spending money, love, sex, excess of anything, absolutely nothing could fill my void or give me the self-worth and value that I was seeking so desperately, until I met Jesus Christ. When I submitted to His will and allowed Him to love me when I did not feel loveable, that is when I began to feel loved.

The Lord knew my plight. He knew what I needed. He led me to the place that would teach me what I needed to learn how to get "un-stuck" from the place in my arrested emotional development. He knew that if I did not emotionally grow, I could never learn to receive Him in a real and meaningful way that would change my life in the way that I needed it to change. I could not receive his love to its fullest until I learned to love myself. I could not learn to love myself, until I could feel forgiven for my wrong doings and to know that I no longer had to live in the shame of my past.

People have a nasty habit of judging one another. We make people feel shame for things they have done. We tend to place varying degrees of severity upon different sins as though we have a right to say which sin is worse than another. The we say how someone should be punished for that sin as though we have the right to do that as well. We tend to want to bash others for what they have done wrong, but want all the grace and mercy God will give us when want absolution from our sins. Selfish human beings, we tend to be. Shame keeps us hidden from God. We are ashamed to face him and accept responsibility for what we have done. If only we would realize that God is so much more forgiving than humans are. He will forgive the moment we repent! He does not want to be separated from us. He wants to be close to us, to love us, and to forgive us, if we will only allow Him to.

The more I learned to love God, the further away I would drift from my sins. I did not want to hurt God. My sins were hurtful to me and I knew they were hurtful to Him as well. When you respect someone, you will not want to hurt them. That is how I feel about God. I do not want to hurt Him or disappoint Him ever, even though I do sometimes. When I do, I apologize and I try again to do things right. God does not expect perfection from us. He expects us to try and try again.

Natural transformation begins when you change behaviors because you love and respect someone, especially God. We want our heavenly Father to be proud of us. Why would we want to continue our self-destructive behaviors when we know that it hurts our Creator, who sacrificed so much for us?

Skills learned here are only tools to use and are helpful in our quest to grow and learn. It is what our physical and emotional part of our body needs to heal old wounds. Jesus is the life blood that feeds our spirit and heals the area of our life that will allow us to receive and give love. He also gives us purpose in life. He tells us to go and make disciples of all nations. When we bring all of this together into a convergence of healing, the light within us becomes brighter for all the world to see.

Love is the answer and God is Love. Be healed emotionally, physically, mentally and spiritually and grab the hand of God and receive His Love through the debt paid for us by His Only Son, Jesus Christ. God sacrificed so much so that you could live happily ever after in eternity.

Romans 10:9 "If you confess with your mouth that "Jesus is Lord", and believe in your heart that God raised Him from the dead, you will be saved!" (NIV)

If you make this decision for your life, I urge you to find a good Bible based church to attend. This is a crucial step in mentorship, growth and learning. Follow the example of Jesus and emulate His every move. He mentored His disciples for three years. He wanted them to be strong enough to stand upon their own two feet when they went out and ministered to others on their own. He knew that they would be going up against the enemy and the principalities of darkness. He knew that they needed to be fully equipped for mission when they went out. He wanted them to be ready.

The disciples taught and served others while traveling with Jesus. They had His oversight and His strength to help guide and guard them as they learned. Jesus planted twelve seeds. He watered them, nurtured them, and cultivated them. Two thousand years later, we still talk about every seed Jesus planted. Jesus spoke to a few big crowds, but He focused on twelve men whom He called and He qualified. With their help, Jesus changed the world. I guess you could say that He planted vertically even though He could see the whole horizontal picture. My prayer is that you too will accept Jesus as your Savior, teacher, mentor and friend. Be healed and become the light to a very darkened world.

Do not allow depression, self-loathing, shame and despair keep you from receiving all that God wants to give to you. You are His child. His desire is to love you and to share with you all that He has. Give Him a chance. Will life be perfect once you do? No. There is nothing perfect this side of heaven. We will have peace of mind knowing that when we do go to heaven that we will no longer suffer what we have here. We will have confidence that we are no longer walking alone through the things we suffer silently in our isolation. God walks with us, and when things are bad, He carries us. I took the chance and am so glad that I did. I hope you will too.

CHAPTER 11

IDENTITY CRISIS

THIS LAST TESTIMONY I am sharing, is to explain how important it is to know who we are. If you don't know, then you need to find out. Our identities are important. Teenagers struggle with figuring it out through adolescence. Eventually, they will figure things out and can move on with their lives searching their purpose and direction. But what happens when we do not know our identity? How can we move forward? How does it affect our lives?

This testimony is out of chronological order from the other testimonies because it started when I was 18-years-old and did not end until 2 years ago. I know that this is an emotionally charged situation for many people that I know and love. For years, I felt I was the only one that hurt. I was in so much pain and despair that I could not see the pain and despair of others. For this I am sorry. I am so grateful for the love of those who did not give up on me as I wandered through it all trying to figure things out.

One day my mom wanted to explain to me about a situation that had been kept secret for many years. She felt it was time to share it due to circumstances which had arose. She proceeded to tell me that I had another sister by my dad. That, in of itself would not have been so upsetting, but the circumstances behind this information was. She then explained that the mother of our sister was someone close to us. She went on to tell me who she was. I became quite upset. In fact, so upset that I raised my voice because we had grown up with this little girl for many years in our lives, but never knew she was our sister. We lived with her for quite a few years. I could not believe what I was hearing. It was wrong, I felt. How could this have been kept from us? I could not wrap my mind around what I perceived to be lies.

I continued to rant about how we could have bonded with her differently, had we known her relationship to us. If we had known her identity, we would have treated her more like family or the sister that she was to us. I felt hurt for both myself and my newly discovered sister. How could anyone do that to her, I asked. Mom explained that the mother wanted to keep it unknown for her own reasons. Back then I could not understand why. Now, with the training that I have obtained and my growth and maturity of years, I have gained the insight to fully understand why. I was a bit hurt that mom would not tell us kids, but I understand now that it was not her secret to tell. This did not keep me from continuing my rant of opinions. I had a powerful sense of justice, and still do today. This situation, to me, was unjust.

Mom continued to listen to me and I could tell she was upset as well, but quietly she listened to what I had to say. She finally broke her silence. Mom asked me if all that I had said to her, was truly how I felt? I was so angry. I blurted out that it sure was! She then said to me, "Sit down, I have something more I need to tell you." I was so upset already that I had too much adrenaline rushing through me to sit down. I told her, "I can't sit, just tell me what it is!" She quietly said that though my sister belonged to my dad biologically, that I however, did not. The only man I knew to be my father, now was not!

There is an old saying, "You could have heard a pin drop." I know firsthand what that sounds like. For a moment, there was deafening silence. I recall smiling nervously and telling mom that she was lying, because she wanted me to feel how my sister felt. I believed that she was trying to teach me a lesson here. I was so wrong. There were many lessons to be learned from all of this, but that was not one of them.

It was not until my mom began to cry, that I realized, she was telling me the truth. I kept saying, "You are kidding, right?" She shook her head "no" and apologized. She continued to cry. I suddenly had an intensity of emotion that I had never felt before. Anger like I had never experienced went through the roof. I felt hot all over and all I could do is pace and try to think a moment. Racing thoughts filled my head and then they just started blurting out. How? Why? Who? These rolled off my tongue faster than mom could answer. I would go from wanting to know the full story, to feeling a tremendous loss.

A few moments ago, I knew who I was. Yes, I had gained a sister, but I knew who I was. Now in this moment, not only had I lost a sister, but I lost another brother who I called Bobby who was my dad's son. Even worse, I had just lost my dad! I lost a whole family on my dad's side. I had just lost my identity! I no longer knew who I was. This caused a huge rift in my relationship with my mother for many years, for which I am extremely sorry. We maintained relationship with one another, I loved her very much and still do. I simply did not know what to do with the information I had just received or all the emotions that I was feeling. I had trusted my mother and I told her, "If you cannot trust your mother, who can you trust?" I felt that my mom had breached a sacred trust and I just could not get over it. I lacked the skills to do it. I was to stay in the victim mentality for way too many years. Wasted years.

Everyone in my dad's family knew the truth, but no one ever told. They had accepted my adoption as if I was always meant to be theirs and no questions asked. I was loved. I loved this family very much. To learn at this stage in my life that their blood was not my blood was devastating to me. I became so focused on my feelings, my hurt, and my pain, that I never once considered the pain of anyone else. I was very selfish at this moment in my hurt. I could not see past me and what I was feeling. I did not care what anyone else was feeling. I really didn't think that anyone else felt anything in the same way that I was. I was having a pity party and I was the queen of the party. Not to minimize the situation, because it was a notable change in my life. I just could not get over it.

It never occurred to me my mom's situation in all of this. She was raised by her grandmother who was born in the late 1800's. Being pregnant out of wedlock was not something that you did and back then, it brought great shame upon a family. Mom was told she should marry my dad to give me a name, because the biological father was not able to do so. Then, there was my dad to consider, who I had had a fallen out with recently. My immaturity was shining through big time. I called him and told him how much I loved him and how sorry I was for my behaviors. I told him that I had such a profound respect for him, more now than ever, because he didn't have to love me, but chose to love me. Suddenly, the pettiness of our falling out was so insignificant compared to this news.

Dad was so upset that mom had told me. The fear he had within him immediately came out, "You are not going to go and find your real father, are you?" He did not want to lose me as his daughter. We cried on the phone together. I told dad I did not know what I would do yet. I was so blown away by this news. I could not think. Then there was the biological father. Who was he? Where was he? Why didn't he want me? How did he feel? As the days went onward, I needed to have answers.

By mom's account, my biological father was young and had a troubled life. He had been in a youth detention center. My mother and I both struggle with pride issues. Mom stated that when she went to visit my biological father to tell him she was pregnant, that he questioned if I was his or not. She said that she was so hurt by that statement, that she got up and left. She never went back or looked back. It was over. I could not understand that. How could she just walk away and not try and convince him that I was his? She had not been with anyone else intimately. It hurt her for him to believe otherwise.

Mom decided to marry Les when he asked mom to marry him. His name was placed on my birth certificate. He became my dad and that was the end of that, so they all thought. My mom told me that she fully intended to go to her grave never telling me. Back then, I wished she hadn't told me, but now I am glad that she did.

It has taken me many years to figure out who I am. No one knew how to help me through this identity crisis. I didn't know how to help myself. I think, had we known how to deal with the situation better, I would not have blamed my mother for so many of my own short comings through the years. My mother is amazing. I love her dearly. I spent entirely too many years in self-pity wanting my mom to pay and hurt as much as I was. Little did I know that she was hurting all along. She loved me. No parent wants to intentionally hurt their child. Mom was no different. I just couldn't see it back then.

I spent the next 20 years searching for my biological father John. The next day after I had found out about him I decided that I would do the "rational thing" and call every John S. in the Denver Metropolitan Phone Book. There were a ton of them in there too! I called every one of them. I had his name, but it was a common name. I was stubborn and I was not giving up. I was going to find him and there was no stopping me, so I thought. I was so depressed, sad and lost that I did not realize how foolish it was for me to call every John S. that I could find in the phone book. What if I did happen to find him that way? He could just say he wasn't my father. I had such a tormented mind at that time. I had to find him. I had to know who I was. I had lost my identity. I felt hopelessly lost forever, it seemed. I did not think I would ever find me again.

I never found John that day, though my fingers were sore from dialing a rotary phone. I can laugh about it now. I searched relentlessly for years. I came close a few times. I had discovered where he may have lived via finding his driver license information. I sent a letter to John in San Jose, California, but I did not get a response back. More questions in my mind emerged. Does he have a new family? Does he want to hear from me? Has he moved? Maybe he didn't leave a forwarding address. Maybe someone else got the letter and didn't tell him about it? I finally gave up. My dad Les, was relieved. I think my mom was too, though she supported every effort that I had made.

I spent so many years feeling sorry for myself. I felt that I no longer had my core five siblings that I was once full blood with. It tormented my mind as well. They didn't act any different toward me the day after I had found out we no longer shared the same father, then they did the day before I had found out. They loved me the same and still do. They were so supportive of me and constantly tried to assure me that nothing was different. But I felt different inside. I felt like I no longer belonged. I could not stand up with the same convictions that I did before about things because I did not have that blood to back me, I felt. I might get rejected now somehow, I believed. I was so wrong. I just could not see it then. I felt that my mom was the only connection that I now had to my own identity. She was it. She was all that I had to who I was or would ever be.

Never once, did I stop to consider, that the love my dad had for me gave me an identity. Nor the fact, that his adopting me gave me an identity. Never once, did I realize, that my main identity was through my Father God in heaven, who created my very being and breathed life into my body with His Spirit. Never, did I once, consider that when I accepted Jesus Christ as my Savior that He was now my identity. The same blood that flows through Jesus, now flows through me. I was a child of God, but could not see it.

All I could see was what I had lost. I could not see what I had gained. My focus was skewed. My vison was blurry. My heart was broken. I knew I just had to find John to discover who I was. He was the key to knowing who I was.

Years passed and I had adjusted some. Occasionally, I would have a melt down and then move on for a while. My mother one day, in a heated argument with me, finally did the right thing by me. She told me that she was no longer carrying this burden. She told me that she had asked God to forgive her, and he did. She had learned to forgive herself. She had begged my forgiveness and I had refused. She said, it was my issue now. If I wanted to heal, I needed to face it and let it go she proclaimed. She would not accept my blaming her any longer. Rightfully so. I know it was difficult for mom to have said that to me, but I needed to hear it.

Oh, I was so angry for her saying that! I so needed to hear it, though I didn't want to hear it. She was right. I had to stop being the victim and heal. I just did not know how. At least until Life Skills came into my life a few years later.

In 2014, my dad Les, came back to the United States to visit. He had moved to Costa Rica to live out his dream. I hated his being so far away, but he was happy. His health was failing, it became evident when he arrived at my home. He was on oxygen and even with it on, he struggled for every breath he took. I was very concerned.

He spent a month with me. At that time, I was living in Denver. We decided that we would go to Kansas so that he could see some of his other kids and grandchildren. The trip was very hard on him. I struggled to keep his oxygen saturation up. He refused to go to the hospital, though I tried to get him to go numerous times.

I believe that he knew that his time for this world was short. He had made out a Last Will and Testament and he wanted to go over it with me. My brother and I were to share as executors of his Will. I did not want to discuss it but I knew that dad was right. Time was limited. I did not want to face the thought of losing him, but I had to. We did briefly discuss what he needed my brother and I to do when the time comes.

One day as he was walking through the living room and I was walking past him to go to the other room, he grabbed my arm and stopped me. He looked at me in a very solemn, sad face. He had tears in his eyes. He said, "Vera, promise me that you will find Bobby (his son who he had not seen since he was 2-years old). Tell him I love him. I always did, and I always will." I knew that dad knew, that this was to be his last trip home. I looked at him and began to cry. "I promise dad. I will find him." He then shook off the pain of his heartache and said, "Good then." And he went and laid down. I cried out to God, "Lord, I am not ready to lose my dad." The thought of his dying was beyond my comprehension.

The day came for him to go back to Costa Rica. We had to put him in a wheel chair so that he could get him to the plane. The Airport would not allow me to park my vehicle there where we had unloaded him and they brought the wheelchair to pick him up. They made me go and park the car so that I could go to see him off down by security. I was trying to hurry so I said, "I will see you in a minute dad. I will be right back." He said, "Okay honey." I jumped in the car and parked it downstairs two levels from where he was. I ran back up to the Airline where I had left him and I could not find anyone. It was late at night. I ran to where they do the safety checks as people go through security, and I saw my little sister who had rode with me to see dad off. She came up with a flat look on her face. "I'm so sorry Vera, they made him board the plane."

I was so upset. I said, "What do you mean they made him board? We are early? I did not get to say good-bye to him!" I began to cry. My sister hugged me and said that they did not have the help to sit and wait on me to park the car. They needed to get him on board. I was devastated. I knew it would be my last time to say good bye to him or to ever feel his hug, to say that I loved him in person. How could this be? I needed my daddy at that moment, one last time. I cried a lot that night.

Then the dreaded day came the last of August 2014, when I got the call from Costa Rica that my dad has passed away. I held it together in front of my husband for the most part and while on the phone with my step-mom, but when I got by myself, I screamed out to God in total agony. I had never known this kind of pain. I had lost grandparents that devastated me, but this was far worse than any grief I had ever experienced. And what made matters worse, was there was to be no real closure. My dad had Willed his body to science and it would remain in Costa Rica. I could not have that moment to sit with him and make it a reality to my mind. We ended up having a small memorial service in Kansas where all my siblings but Bobby who we had not yet found, came to share in one another's grief. I was living in Arkansas by this time.

After I returned to Arkansas from the memorial service, I was consumed with grief. I was not coping well. I was having panic attacks and depression like none I had ever felt before. I was not sharing this with anyone but my sister Ruth. She and I tried hard to heal by leaning on one other. It was a challenging time for all my siblings one way or another. I had always been the one that others relied upon in times of need and now I was useless. I could not sleep. I would work all night and then lay in bed thinking all day when I should be sleeping. Sometimes I would sit on the back porch looking toward Costa Rica crying out to my dad telling him how sorry I was for every rotten nasty word I had ever spoken to him. I would then cry out to God for him to heal this pain I was feeling. "Just take it away Lord! Please! Take it away! I cannot handle this!" I felt that God was not listening to me. I felt so abandoned and alone.

One day my Aunt Barb called me. She had found a woman on Facebook that was willing to search for my brother Bobby. Aunt Barb had recalled that I had made dad a promise to find him. We did not know his last name for sure. I had a picture of him from when he was last living with us and he was about 2-years-old, I had guessed. I figured by now he was in his forties. We gave what little information we did have to a woman named Susan who lived in Tulsa, Oklahoma. She got on it.

Susan called me one day and said, "Guess what? I think I have found him!" She sent me a picture of him. I took one look and I said, "Oh my gosh! He looks like dad!" I knew it was him. She asked if I wanted to call him. I was afraid of messing things up because I was so emotional having just lost dad. I explained that to her. I also told her that I felt that she needed a little more background, so that she could explain some things to Bobby in case he refused to talk to us. I told her that he was not actually my blood, but he was my legal brother through adoption. Saying that broke my heart. I had always dreamed of the day I would hug my baby brother again and a lot of water had run under the bridge since then, including losing my blood connection I always thought I had. I had always believed that "blood was thicker than water" as I had always heard. Another Life Commandment.

The woman was intrigued with my story. She asked if I had ever tried to find my real father? I told her I had, but that I gave up years ago. She asked me what his name was out of curiosity and a few other questions. We chit-chatted a while and then she said that she would make the call to my brother.

I was so excited to hear that Bobby was cautiously willing to make an initial connection with me. He wanted to know what I had hoped to gain by this re-connection. I just wanted him to know we were here for him, we loved him and most importantly I needed to fulfill my promise to my dad. He could not share the same emotions as I had because he was so little when he left and had no recollection of any of us. He was genuinely sorry for my loss of dad. He had a strong connection with his adoptive father, much like I had with mine. Bobby's blood line was my world, but it was not necessarily his. Understandably so.

My sister Ruth and I finally went to meet Bobby later that year in Oklahoma for lunch. I did not want to let go of him. I hugged him so tight. It was like hugging dad, or at least a piece of him. I felt so blessed to have found him. In my mind's eye, it was like hugging my brother as he was when I last seen him at age two. Words cannot express the happiness and excitement that both Ruth and I felt that day.

I think it helped both Ruth and me, finding him. It was like spiritual medicine given straight from God himself. Some happiness creeped back into our lives during a very dark time. Bobby was healing a torn heart and had no idea that he was. We did not realize ourselves how the presence of our baby brother could help to relieve some of the pain of the grief and loss we both had been suffering. We praised God for allowing us to find him. What a blessing from God in our time of need!

Not long after this reunion with Bobby, I received a phone call from Susan. She wanted to know how things went with meeting my brother. I told her it was great and thanked her again. She said, "Well, I have another surprise for you." I said, "Oh yeah? What is that?" She then proceeded to tell me that she had found my biological father John. I could not believe what I was hearing. I had not told her to look for him. She felt compelled to do it on her own. I did not know how to feel at first. I felt tremendous guilt initially. My dad never wanted me to find my father. I felt that I was betraying him, especially since he had just died. I felt that I was betraying my siblings during their time of grief. I was betraying the whole family for that matter, in my mind. I did not know what to do.

My sister Ruth was living with me in Arkansas at that time. Like I said, she and I were grieving together. She knew how bad I was taking dad's death and she felt that my having this new connection would help me. In her wisdom, she said that maybe God was allowing this to happen now, so that John could be my surrogate father to help me through the loss of dad. God can send us light in our times of need. I needed someone to take my focus off dad's death and bring some type of happiness to my life again. But what if John was not someone that would allow that? Then I would only be bringing more grief into my life, I thought to myself. I was afraid to make the wrong decision.

Ruth was persistent. She insisted that I was not betraying anyone. John was my blood and I needed to at least make an initial contact. If I did not feel that it could go any further after speaking to him, then I could stop the contact. I told Susan to go ahead and make the initial contact because I was fearful of the rejection I might receive. I was so afraid of rejection. In my mind, I believed that he never wanted to see me and this could get ugly. Or, what if he had a wife that did not know about me? I did not want to upset his family. I did not want to be the reason an innocent family might fall apart. So many scenarios played out in my mind. Then it occurred to me that I could possibly have more siblings out there. Some brothers, some sisters, or maybe both! I also wanted to know or rediscover my root of who I am. My heart won over my logic and fear this day.

Susan made the call. She then called me back all excited. Yes, it was him! She stated that he had been looking for me for the past three years. He wanted to talk to me. My world was in a crazy spiral and I did not know which end was up. I had so many emotions, thoughts, concerns, worries, and my list went on and on. My mother had seemed a bit distant after I told her we found him. I later found out that she too was having the same anxiety that I was. She never thought I would find him. Mom had believed that, this part of her life was buried and gone. Yet, here it was resurrecting before her eyes. She had lots of things to resolve as well from her past. She and I worked it out together.

The first call that came to me was John's sister, my Aunt Mary. She was so excited and just could not express how elated that she and their family were that they found me. She gave me a little family history and basically helped to break the ice for me and my father. I think my father was as nervous as I was about all of this too. He used his sister as I had used Susan, to enter an emotional piece of our lives that we did not know what to expect. We both needed a buffer. Thanks to both Susan and Mary, they were willing to be navigators for this amazing reunion.

Then the much-anticipated call came from my father. I cannot tell you the overwhelming emotions that I felt when I heard his voice and realized that the ghost of my mother's past was alive and

I now have found my identity. The peace that came rushing over me was amazing. I had some reconciliation within myself by just hearing his voice. Over numerous phone calls I learned about who I was, what my blood line was and why he had allowed some other man to adopt me without a fight.

Even though I knew his birthdate all along, it never dawned on me that he was a young man of only 17-years-old when I was born. There are not many 17-year-old boys that are prepared or ready to be fathers at that age. John was no exception. He was having turbulent teen problems and he could not be the father that he felt he should be or that I needed. He told me that he knew the man that was adopting me. He knew him to be a good man. He said, though it was hard for him to let go, he knew that it was the right thing to do for me. He validated everything my mother had said. He never said one harsh word about my mother or my dad. I believe that his questioning mom's fidelity was more out of his fear of being a father so young. He was not ready and he knew it.

John had accepted responsibility for everything that happened that caused our separation from each other. Immediately, my heart swelled with a new love for a man that I did not even know. It is hard to be mad at someone who accepts responsibility for their actions and holds themselves into account. I was developing respect for this man.

Two years after finding John, he continues to call me every couple of weeks to check on me. Though our talks may lack some depth sometimes because we have yet to meet one another, it is a treasured moment each time he calls. He puts out effort to have a relationship with me. I view it as love. He sends Christmas money for his great-grandkids each year too. I have not met him as of this writing, but I hope to meet him someday soon. I have grown to respect his hard life and words of wisdom, because I too have learned the hard way. It's funny how we have a lot in common. I did find out that I have three more brothers and I look forward someday to meeting them as well. In fact, I have a huge family on my father's side to one day meet and love.

Finding John brought closure to my identity crisis and in many ways made me aware that I always had an identity. I just did not realize where it came from or who I was. My earthly identity came from my biological parents and from Les, my dad who adopted me. However, the greatest identity I possess is the identity of my Creator, Abba, Father God. Had I just realized that long ago, I would have not squandered so many years being the victim and trying to make my mother pay for my pain. But regrets only waste more years, so I will learn this lesson and move on. I will just love the new dad I have in my life, cherish my mother whom I adore, be thankful for my dad Les, who helped create the character of who I am within me and praise God for my identity. For in and through all of them combined, I am, who I am.

You do not have to be adopted to have this type of struggle. However, adoption does add to the confusion no matter how much the adoptive person or persons love you. It is not a reflection on the adoptive parents, but on the contrary, an internal conflict of identity and a quest to know who we, the adopted, are as human beings. Knowledge of truth does set you free from the bondage. I am a firm believer that if a child is raised in the truth of the situation from which they came, that they will emerge much more successfully into adulthood, than they would have had they not known the truth.

Of course, I am willing to help others that I may find in an analogous situation as I was in, to discover their identity and restore healing in their hearts to the best of my ability. What a shame it would be if I refused to help others through the things they are going through, knowing I may have the answers they are searching for. If you or I have been through something that has made us wiser, we absolutely need to share it with others.

If you have accepted Jesus Christ as your Savior and struggle to know who you are, whether because of an absent parent, or because of your believing you are a nobody, the truth is about to unfold. If you have not accepted Jesus as your Savior, then the same truth is about to unfold for you as well. It might be just the truth you need to know to make that decision between you and God.

Fact is, God is our Creator. He breathed life into our bodies. His breath is His Spirit and life inside of our bodies. Our Spirits will someday return to be with Him, or they will spend eternity separated from Him. It is completely our choice given to us by the gift of free will. Because He is our Creator, that makes us His family. Being in His family gives us an Identity. We come from Royalty. God is the King of all Kings! We come from a strong blood line that can tear down strongholds! We are sons and daughters of the Most High God, Maker of heaven and earth. Learn these solid truths I am about to reveal to you, that were given to me. Study them, memorize them as a positive self-talk, make your brain believe the truth! Why? Because the truth can set you free! (John 8:32)

You are who God says that you are. You will be able to stand up with boldness and conviction and know that your daddy, Abba Father, has your back! We are family! Know who you are!

I AM . . .

1. A child of God (Romans 8:16)
2. Redeemed from the hand of the enemy (Psalms 107:2)
3. Forgiven (Colossians 1:13, 14)

4. Saved by Grace through Faith (Ephesians 2:8)
5. Justified (Romans 5:1)
6. Sanctified (1 Corinthians 6:11)
7. A new Creature (II Corinthians 5:17)
8. Partaker of His Divine Nature (II Peter 1:4)
9. Redeemed from the Curse of the Law (Galatians 3:13)
10. Delivered from the power of darkness (Colossians 1:13)
11. Led by the Spirit of God (Romans 8:14)
12. A son (daughter) of God (Romans 8:14)
13. Kept in safety wherever I go (Psalms 91:11)
14. Getting all my needs met by Jesus (Philippians 4:19)
15. Casting all my cares on Jesus (1 Peter 5:7)
16. Strong in the Lord and in the Power of His Might (Ephesians 6:10)
17. Doing all things through Christ Who strengthens me (Philippians 4:13)
18. An heir of God and a joint-heir with Jesus (Romans8:17)
19. Heir to the blessings of Abraham (Galatians 3:13, 14)
20. Observing and doing the Lord's Commandments (Deuteronomy 28:12)
21. Blessed coming in and going out (Deuteronomy 28:6)
22. An inheritor of eternal life (1 John 5:11, 12)
23. Blessed with all spiritual blessings (Ephesians 1:3)
24. Healed by His Stripes (1 Peter 2:24)
25. Exercising my authority over the enemy (Luke 10:19)
26. Above only and not beneath (Deuteronomy 28:13)
27. More than a conqueror (Romans 8:37)
28. Establishing God's Word here on earth (Matthew 16:19)
29. An overcomer by the Blood of the Lamb and Word of my Testimony (Rev.12:11)
30. Daily overcoming the devil (1 John 4:4)

31. Not moved by what I see (II Corinthians 4:18)
32. Walking by Faith and not by sight (II Corinthians 5:7)
33. Casting down vain imaginations (II Corinthians 10: 4, 5)
34. Brining every thought into captivity (II Corinthians 10:5)
35. Being transformed by a renewed mind (Romans 12:1, 2)
36. A laborer together with God (1 Corinthians 3:9)
37. The righteousness of God in Christ (II Corinthians 5:21)
38. An imitator of Jesus (Ephesians 5:1)
39. The light of the world (Matthew 5:14)
40. Anointed with Fresh Oil (Psalms 92:10)

As we learned in our skills section, our brains won't initially believe what we are telling it. It believes contrary to truth because of false life commandments. But we will control what we can control. We have the skill and the ability to change the programming. We will say the verses until we believe them. We then will go and help others believe the truth about themselves. This is truly setting the captives free.

Do not fear what others will say about you when you share the truth of the Gospel. I have been called a fanatic and even hyper-religious at times. That is just fine by me. I have been called worse.

I am a Denver Bronco fan. I have been to games where people were screaming and yelling for their teams. True NFL fans have already defined the word fanatic. I also scream and yell like a fanatic for the Broncos. No one thought it strange for me to cheer on my team to victory, unless they did not like the Broncos. People scream and cheer across this nation for their favorite teams, whether in the stadium or at home in front of the television. There is no shame screaming for our favorite team as we cheer them on to victory. It is a time of fun and unity.

Why then should we be shamed for cheering on God's team? There should be no shame in screaming for God, rooting people onward toward God or celebrating a "touch down" when someone accepts Christ as their savior! We should be ecstatic when someone over powers the grave and receives the gift of eternal life! So much more is at stake in this "game" than that of the NFL. Your very soul and Spirit are counting on you to make the right choice. That is something to shout about. When someone makes the right choice, it is victory!

We should all be equally as boisterous for Christ, as we are our home town teams. Do not be ashamed to love God openly. Jesus said that if we are ashamed of Him before man, that He would be ashamed of us before His Father in Heaven (Mark 8:38). Choose this day whom you shall serve! The world will always fail you, God will not.

Learn to help others to navigate the darkness and emerge as light. Give your life purpose.

I now pass this ember of light to ignite your torch. Will you accept it? I pray so. Now, may your darkness fade and your light shine brightly all the days of your life with purpose and love into all eternity! May God, bless you in your walk and in your new transformation. May His love be a lamp unto your feet, and a light upon your path. May God, give you clear and unwavering determination to finish the race. Upward and homeward bound. In Jesus name, Amen.

Made in the USA
Columbia, SC
12 July 2021